Let Us Pretend Caregiving is Easy

Mab Morris

This book is dedicated to all caregivers.

www.mabmorris.com

ISBN: 979-8-9951926-4-0

Contents

Preamble

The first year of my stay at my mother's house, the private FB Group Caregivers of Elderly Parents was incredibly helpful. AC, AM, ES, GMY, KF, KK, and several others: THANK YOU. They read many of these poems first. Some of these members I cried for. Some I prayed for. Some I feared for their lives.

My deep thanks to the codependency community led by Marshall Burtcher. Moving home was like entering into codependency bootcamp. He, and others in the group, gave me tools to help me survive, beyond the tools suggested by other caregivers. There were some surprising overlaps in membership.

My deep thanks to Visiting Angels, specifically some of Mom's favorite carers: Nimo, Somaya, and especially, my rocks, Lynda and Jovina. Administrative people who were helpful were Lauren, and Kelly the scheduling queen. You made me feel so very much not alone!

I must note that these poems are only from my perspective.

Years ago, a therapist said that if there are five members of a family, there are five families. We all have our own perspective on that family, our own understanding.

Around year two of my stay, both of my sisters had real reasons for not being able to come and help. One lived only twenty minutes away, the other eight hours. There were times I regretted telling them that twelve, and then eighteen hours "off" were sufficient. It meant I couldn't go home. For over a year, excepting Visiting Angels, I had no other support.

I can't blame my sisters for taking me at my word. I used that thought like gauze to staunch figurative bleeding of the thought: They could choose to come. My life felt like a sacrificial lamb to my mom's caregiving. I can't blame them for any familial fracturing that we all created together.

Love was there, I promise!

However, this is part of the caregiver pain that many experience, and so I won't hide from it. I'm sure there are families where caregiving strengthens bonds. Most of the time it reveals the lack thereof.

The order of poems I curated by date.

I chose to curate the poems not by theme, but by the date. It felt—even as I added addendums when I'd revise and edit the poems—as if it had its own tension, its own reason for being, its own story to tell. I added some prose to the mix as well.

Overall: This shares moments in one woman's journey in caregiving her beloved mother. It includes poems about others I either cared for, or inspired by stories I heard from others.

Part One

Let's Pretend

Let us pretend
That the plants I bought
Says that this is my home now.
That they mean it.
It's not just another of these
Falsehoods building up the walls
For the home that is not mine.
Plants, music, food,
Pictures from home, a toothbrush,
My favorite dish soap,
A closet filled with my clothes,
And the choice to not leave
To care for someone who needs it...
Let us pretend that it is always easy
And that the plant,
And a toothbrush, and a closet filled with clothes
Makes me believe it is so.

—Thursday 31 December 2020

A Moment of Prose: Fall Risk

July 6, 2019: Fall. Displaced femoral neck fracture. Surgery. Recovery.

October 14, 2020: Second fall. Hit head. Helped up. No medical intervention.

November 21, 2020: Third fall. Hit head. Blood on the floor. Could not get up without EMT help.

Mom refused to let my twin—who lived nearby—call for EMTs. I came in after an hour and a half of a frantic drive from my own home. I demanded Mom get checked out. Two hours of stubbornness, tears, and handwringing:

Our lives... *my* life would never be the same.

In the Autumn of 2019, before my mother came home from rehab, after she'd broken her hip, she'd insisted on going to her bedroom downstairs. The bathroom nearby worked minimally at best. She had a choice of staying, or coming home. Instead of being on the main floor, with working bathrooms, the kitchen, her favorite chair, she insisted on keeping things normal, gimpy hip or not.

With the social worker threatening to keep her there, there was a flurry, and scurry to get the house ready for her, safe for her. We discovered the septic system had been neglected for about fifty years, made worse because Mom planted shrubberies in the drain field. While she was in rehab, we had to get it connected to the sewer system.

Three sisters breathed a bit, but all dubious about the need for a woman barely recovered from a left hip hemiarthroplasty to do those stairs. Mom insisted, with vigor.

Her three daughters retreated into our own refuges, our own homes, and licked our own wounds, and calmed our minds.

I went back to driving seventy miles down, once a week, to buy her groceries then back again. It included a container of blueberries. She'd count out ten for her cereal every other day. I also bought her wine, and so many other things that brought her comfort in the set, steady—comfortable and safe!—schedule of her life. A daily routine of just sitting in her turnable rocking chair, watching the few neighbors of this dead-end street.

When she fell again, in October 2020, I stayed for a week, to help with her anxiety, the first cause of her fall risk: the sense of being unsteady leading to a fear of falling, and thus not moving, exercising to combat the weakness that would make a fall inevitable.

I prepared to come and stay. We'd long talked about it. I'd cared for elders before. I was the one sister who could work from home. Surely helping her wouldn't impact that. *Little did I know!*

The first night after the third fall, in November, I helped her down the stairs. Her anxiety was so high, she couldn't go all the way without having to sit down. I held her, and promised her that she'd never have to do the stairs again.

She sagged in my arms with relief.

This was a surprise to me. I thought she'd fight me. Her tension, however, drained out of her. She'd been holding on to independence with every fiber of her being—regardless of her fears.

The following weeks, I slowly moved in for a long stay, my daughters bringing me boxes, when I couldn't.

She was a fall risk, with high blood pressure—because she would only take her blood pressure when she felt like it: a theme. If the side effects of any medication had the word dizzy in it, it was inevitable she'd refuse and complain. I guided her to drink only 8 ounces of wine a night, instead of a bottle. The idea of being both tippy and tipsy, and the memory of those stairs, still makes me shudder.

Slowly I was forced to take over her bills, and insisted she get a will updated. I became her power of attorney. Anxiety, High Blood Pressure, and Fall Risk?

I was there. She no longer had to count blueberries. I poured them over her cheerios and her oatmeal squares with abandon.

102 and Linen

I iron old linen
While Dorothy sits nearby.
The cloth holds the memory of wrinkles
Neither steam nor sizing
Can smooth out.
Dorothy counts numbers.
She just likes them, she told me.
Counting, and touching
The teddy bear she holds comforts her.
I remember she was a textile artist
And show her the delicate lace and linen.
She tells me I'm doing a nice job.
I iron; she counts, then says,
"I hope..."
I kneel before her when she stops.
"Hope what?"
"I hope it turns out nice."
"I'm trying," I tell her. "Linen is stubborn."
"It's a little bit stubborn," she tells me.
"Just a little."
I think of her age: one hundred and two,
And how white gold linen with intricate lace
Holds the memory of wrinkles
That sizing and steam
Should never smooth out.

—Friday 18 April 2014

Memories Ripped in Half

She sat at her old piano
Forgetting it was hers, and the hours
She'd put her fingers to the keys
With music and students.
Now, all she knows: It is out of tune.
What songs play in her mind
As her children divide memories,
Going through the house,
And cut up their own:
One gets this, another gets that...
And a childhood memory gets ripped in half.
They cannot take a chainsaw to the furniture–
You have this leg,
Here's the drawer–
And grieve as someone takes that table home.
Your memory isn't greater than mine!
Better than mine.
I wanted that! What if I don't remember?

And the woman at the piano
Forgets the house is hers,
Memories fractured, lost and forgotten,
She sits at the piano
Content.
The music still endures,
Though the piano is out of tune.

—Thursday 17 April 2014

How to Say Yes

She fills her cup only halfway
And the stains on the carpet
Speak of her passing
Back and forth, plate and cup
She can do this slow passage
From one space to the next
And each grind of the joints
That slows her down each day
Daily attention and adjustment
Slower and slower, as her coffee cup
Gets filled lower and lower
Without dripping a line of passage
From one room to the next
Along the line of her walker's
Cycling along the carpet
Like the sun, and each day's grind
And measure of slowing steps...

—Monday 26 October 2020

Exile

I am home.
I am in exile.
Where was the life
I created?
But here is still familiar.
Yet nothing is
And everything has the tension
Of an alien life.
Familiar, strange...
I want to go back to my own world,
Because childhood is truly gone.

—Monday 30 November 2020

Breathe

Breathe...
My sister once showed me
How to take breaths
Teaching me to play the flute,
My fingers on her old instrument
As she now played the oboe.
And we both needed to
Be able to
Breathe...

I'm showing our mother
This deep breath:
Leaning in a chair,
Taking a deep breath.
Weak breath only moves the shoulders.
You can tell
If you breathe into your belly
The deepest breaths
Lift our bodies
Higher.
Meditation breath 101
Flute wise, oboe wise
I'll try to get Mom's blood pressure down...

Breathe.
I also need to remember
Just to breathe...
My sister showed me... how.

—Tuesday 8 December 2020

Self-Care

I see these exhausted fellows
On their similar journey.
Some have been at this for years,
And I'm not yet a month in.
And I wonder...
When?
When do I hit that point of exhaustion?
Next month? Next year, five, ten?
When it no longer matters
That I'm a writer,
That I have friends...
Will they all fade out each day that I live here,
And one day I'll notice that they're gone?
I'm gone...?
I've given myself away too much,
And all I am is Caregiver,
And the ME who was strong
Was given away,
And that all I've got room for is stress
Exhaustion, and wanting to run away, sleep...
But there's nothing outside
To be found anymore.
I've forgotten how to ask.

Give myself
A moment in the shower—
Make myself shower everyday—
And wash my own skin,
My own self.
And at night, read my own books.
In my journal write my own thoughts.
Buy a treat for me.
Call a friend at random.
So I am always remembering Me
As self care.

Then I will remember I am strong,
Not pretending to be strong,
And there I will survive
All this loving.

—Saturday 19 December 2020

There's an In-House Call Button

She's possibly got three days
To herself
To do her own thing.
I tell her, with delight–
because I understand–
"Enjoy it! I've only had two hours off all month."

"You've had time to yourself!"
Comes the emphatic snarled reply.
"Haven't you?
To meditate, to write, exercise...
All my time
All month is work or headaches or migraines..."

This is true.
But I can't go home.
I'm always on call.

This time to myself is against
That 24/7...
And Mom calls any time.
My time is not my own.

—Wednesday 23 December 2020

Anyway, But More

Make the bed,
Breakfast, coffee, lunch, tea...
Daily chores I'd be doing myself
Anyway!

When did these tasks
Become a job?
When they were done for my mother?
When she claimed I had not made the bed
As I do every morning?
When I wait for her to start
My day... Having prepared
To wait on her
And her infirmity.
Daily chores I'd be doing *anyway*,
But adding her clock to it all:
My clock, my time
Speeding along in a home I have
Far away.
Make coffee, breakfast,
Then the bed,
Her bed, my bed...

There are things she cannot do by herself–
She lived too long alone!–
Will never do again...
Daily chores I'd be doing
Anyway,
But more.

—Wednesday 23 December 2020

White Peace Grief

The water is running
Down my back.
Suddenly I realize:
I closed the bathroom door.

I loved—too much—
The white tiled peace
Of this space.

I cannot do this.
I open the door,
So I can hear the call bell—
Fall risk ever present—
And step back into the
Water's flow
And try to let
This moment's grief drain away—
In "my" space
Where I am never
Quite at peace, and never alone.

—Wednesday 23 December 2020

Refuge

In this white painted room I find refuge
Only a few colors here:
A carpet from my house
A splash of yellow scarf
From a friend.
But the walls are bare.

This is unlike my own home
With paintings by artist friends,
My daughter's artwork on the walls,
Embroidered cloth from other lands,
And miles of books
Displaying a vibrancy of life I created.
A house so full of my life,
No lover could live there, but visit.
And then return me
Back to myself.

Here in a house filled with
My mother, and my mother's life,
I must now live.
I cannot leave, and return her back
To her solitude, and me to mine,
And whatever quiet or vibrancy we choose.
I must make space within it.

In this white room there is calmness
In a new life, where the days are often loud
Not in noise, but worry and care,
And entanglement from the past,
And fears of the future,
Her life and mine.

The tears for the losses
And refuge for whatever gains,
And I find some small space
To myself.

—Thursday 24 December 2020

After Her Second Fall

My mother's door
Looks like the entrance
To a tomb–
I can almost feel the cold of the stone
Stained with darkness and the death
Of neglected plants,
And the moldering taste of stale air
That reminds me of the blood stains
On her carpet from her fall.
I will return to my mother's home,
And shut this door upon us both
A living death as I wait with her
And on her
Because she can no longer live
Alone.
And so doing, say goodbye
To my life:
Friends, projects, landscaping,
Community of writers and artists,
All so far, and unreachable
Beyond that tomb like choice,
And door...

After Her Third Fall

....But my friends reached out,
Saying it is not goodbye.
They refused to let me shut myself in,
And I grabbed at their hands greedily.
I brought them in,
And we sat together with my mother
And brought the light in.
I cleaned the carpet,
And the new plants thrived.
And she is getting stronger.

—Tuesday 29 December 2020

"It Bothers Me!"

All her life she wanted her house neat.
There are no servants
That her mother used to dominate,
Nor the looming weight of her mother's perfection
Gathering up all attention.
All she knows now is that she cannot understand
A misplaced magazine in someone else's home.
"What kind of mind is that? I don't understand it.
It bothers me!"

She cannot understand
The chipped bowl my sister gives to the cat to eat from,
Just thinks of its precious history,
And her china kept safe away in an old sideboard,
Or all the other objects and furniture from her—
Her mother's house—and her mother's past.
I see the future of a long stay.
Having watched, after her third fall,
The confusion of time and place, the strange anger
And the resentment about her beloved husband, her friends
Vile and vicious, like the unruly, random magazines
And chipped plates, and thoughtless disorder...
All rising up as the sun goes down.

The careful protection of her orderly place
Dismantled in the distress of her fall.
Unreal, unreasonable, or once unspoken things
That bothered her.

Her anxiety looms
And dominates my thoughts
As her mother must still do, even now
Reflected in the studied perfection of her house,
But will fade even though she is better,
Because time, and age, will only march on,
Giving rise to all that are a bother.
I work to give her any measure of comfort now
For I have seen what may come.

Reflected in her almost motto like phrase,

"It bothers me."

—Wednesday 30 December 2020

The Blessings of this Grief

I put my foot down
So hard, I could almost feel
The walls of my mother's house shake
And like a ripple of a pond
Where the rock as been thrown,
Or an animation of a tremor on the earth.
I see what has been done.

TALK!
I said. Everyone needs to talk
To each other.
But now the structures
Of this family life
Has gaps I can see through.

When did I learn the language
Of mistrust,
For my sisters?
And I want to dismantle the house
Which built these false "truths"
My mother sometimes clings to.

I want to put my foot down
Again.
So hard, I can feel
The walls of this house shake,
To where I can see through
The clouded windows,
And break the supporting beams
Of all our misunderstandings.

—Wednesday 30 December 2020

Addendum :

I failed to fix
The broken beams.
It was not my job.
I could only focus
On giving care
Within the unseen ruins
Of our family here.

—Thursday 27 April 2023

I Could...

I could leave,
You know. Go back home.
Get a new job,
Survive for three months.

I have a choice
To be here.

My heart cracks
Because she cannot
Live alone.

—Thursday 31 December 2020

Not My First Day

"Are you going to help me get ready for bed?"
Fed up with the repeated questions:
"Yes, Mom, like I do every day," I say.

The caregiver group
Suggest, "It's not my first day."
Or asking questions...
They have experienced repeated demands, even whistles,
Like the call bell I have in Mom's home.
We do it with a smile,
But we go to our safe spaces
In the corners of the house that remain to us
And try not to cry. Or do cry, as quietly as we can.
Made to feel stupid, thoughtless, forgetful,
Neglectful...
But we do this every day.
"Did you fill my water bottle with water?"
She can see the water in it, on her bedside.
"No. Vodka." The flippant comment pops out.
I tremble at the mistake.

"Oh, I'll sleep well tonight."
She laughs.
I laugh, trying not to cry. At least we joked about it.
I go to my room, though, to get ready for bed,
To start it all over the next day.

—Thursday 31 December 2020

Remind Me

Remind me why I'm not drinking on the job?
It would be so easy to drown in that stuff.
I'm sitting in a parking lot thinking about coffee
Thinking about the liquor store just steps away.
But I know that if I drink at Mom's home
Then it would be so easy to never stop.
I would kill myself trying to survive this way.

—Thursday 31 December 2020

Addendum:

And all this is has become...
Just the wish to survive
When all self care tools
Take such efforts to even use.
And drinking does not: I know...
That the false calm is dangerous.

—Thursday 27 April 2023

Just a Pause

There's no place to go
That's not an errand
If I can't go home.
The choice is a parking lot
A plant store
The liquor store...
A park...
But those aren't escapes
Just a pause...
Without any real relief...
Just in the endless pressure
Of someone else's needs.

—Thursday 31 December 2020

Venting, Crying, Laughing

What do we talk about
In our elder caregiver group?

Poop. Lots and lots of poop.
Poop in the pantry,
Or other unexpected places.
And pee, and why do why do they prefer
A bucket, not a bedside potty
Someone else has to dump,
Or smell it all day long...
Support panties.
And why can't they flush?
The endless repeated demands...
How tired we are.
How much we truly love them.
Mourning their lost dignity, and ours.
Venting crying laughing
Finding tips and tricks and tools for the trade,
Why family and friends don't understand,
But we do
The need for headphones...
For them. *We* can't wear those!
Are you crazy: *We'd* never be able to hear them call out!

(Note: The difference between us and those
Who cannot understand our experience).
And THAT is why we are here.
We reach out in this group,
Like a club none of us truly wanted to belong to
And yet we are so very very glad that we do,
Daily grateful for those who *truly* understand.

—Thursday 31 December 2020

Precious

I'm waking this morning,
Trying to see the small—
HUGE victories:
Like Mom washed her face with two hands.
She stood for three minutes.
I watched her cruise around the house
With the PT Therapist, Lee, using a gait belt.
Her BP is averaging only in the 150s,
And we've seen 130s.
She knows she needs help.
Sometimes the good things come with loss,
And really hard work
And frankly they're making me weep right now.
Because I want more of them.
Like Mom getting a banana *herself*
From the kitchen.
It's not that the small victories,
The good things make the loss and hard work worth it—
No, because it doesn't—
It just makes them merely precious.

—Friday 1 January 2021

I don't know who you are...

On her slow, sundering
Deathbed, where memories died first
And one by one the organs
Of her body,
She looked at her daughter
And could not remember her.
"I don't know who you are..."
She could not recall the years of strife
Because her daughter was gay,
The struggle the pain
For them both.
Her daughter forgot all of that too
And brought her mother into her home
To care for her in her slow,
Relentless dying.
"I don't know who you are,"
Her mother said,
"But I think you're someone
I love very much."

—Saturday 2 January 2021

I could finally write this poem,
years after I heard it.

Fourteen Steps

My father would run up the stairs–
Like I do when my mother calls–
He'd run up fourteen steps into her world
To share with her a portion of his passion
Semantics, theology, something he valued.
She would listen, seeming intent upon his words,
Understanding nothing of it.
Yet the gift of sharing, he would hear
What was wrong with his writing, now able to fix it,
And return to his world downstairs.

She calls me, home alert, or cell phone,
I ask what she needs.
"The mailman has come.
You don't have to get it right away."
For weeks, running up those fourteen steps, to listen...
I knew something was wrong in those words.
Interrupted in my own interests–as surely she
Once, must have been–
"You don't have to get it right away,"
Doesn't mean at my leisure,
Interrupted already...but when I am finished with
Whatever it is I am doing... and right after *that*...
A pale gesture of politeness, against the tacit
Agreement that I am now in her world.
What she actually means, "Now. I want it done now."

Between mother and father, and their worlds
Miles apart between fourteen steps,
My presence now, downstairs, seems like a learned thing.
I am as remote as my home seventy miles away.
She calls, again, trying for clarity, trying to give me space.
"When you come up, will you be wearing shoes?"
She cannot say, "The mailman has come,
Will you please get it now?"
I reply, "When I am done with what I am doing..."
(Writing this poem!) "I will put my shoes on..."
And then I will run up fourteen steps,
Leaving my world, my father's former world,
Into hers. And remember that I'm here to do what she
can't...
While it is on her mind.

—Friday 22 January 2021

Oh, that's my jaw

I've been happy.
It was a good day.
But there's a bottle of wine.

Here's the measure of stress...
I feel my jaw unclench.
The sensation of teeth
Up to my ears

And a sense of breathing...
Here is the room to cry...
Oh G*D I want to cry...
But I can't yet.

She is still upstairs.
She still needs care,
And yet my teeth feel
White, whole,
But for a moment I can tell them...
Let go.
Open wide,
Howl, if you cannot laugh.

—Saturday 23 January 2021

Addendum:

I can do neither.
Benign

And this
Is the stress I've been living with
All my life

My shoulders cannot relax.
It is in wine's glass
Where I can see this.

This sturdy tension
Honed over years
Not just a string on some violin,
But a deep corded thing...

But it is benign.
Our life has been good.
The cool glass
Of wine...

But it is all...
Benign.
The rope cords of stress,

With a glass of scotch
Or wine,
And the hum of tension
The tones of music

Like a plucked string
Of a violin.

—Saturday 23 January 2021

Vulnerable

My sister is coming
And she will see all my weakness
Guess at my drinking.
See my mess,
What I do not clean.
Know what I don't do.
The suggestion of dirty laundry
And not just my own.

And yet...

I want her to see,
Reveal myself so she knows
Everything of my life here.

—Saturday 30 January 2021

Addendum, Much Later:

Never again
Will I be this...
Vulnerable
To someone who
Doesn't understand!

Sit at the Table

Mom and I sit at the dinner table.
For the first time in years
She is not sitting in "her chair" for a meal
With her food hovering over her lap,
Plate or bowl at angles that will one day
Become alarming.

I can hear echoes of all the conversations
Growing up… and yet…
Were they actually ever warm?
Intellectual debates,
[Combative politeness, "arguing" of]
Theology, philosophy,
That made the minds of our parent's daughters
Function so high we need
Libraries of books for all our thoughts.
We'd separate to our own rooms
Once the meal was over, to catch our breath,
Find space for our own minds.
Now we escape to our own houses, miles or states apart,
To fill them with our own thinking.

That Mom and I sit at the dining table
Came only with her reluctant acquiescence,
"I'll comply"
To my request
That we sit here for a meal.

And then the relent,
"I like this."
But she fights it, still,
Not wanting to make the effort.

—Monday 1 February 2021

Addendum:

I relented as well,
When the table became hard for her to sit at,
And we ran out of things to say.
So our plates hover over our laps, or hover over a coffee table.
As we watch movies together.

—Thursday 6 April 2023

Entangled

I used to escape all those threads
I could neither fix nor navigate
And they'd catch upon my ankles...

But I closed my eyes
And pretended it was merely a net
To catch my fall.

Because now,
I'm here by choice.

Family, the concept...
Cannot find a home here.
Where to find the "We" in all this,
Knowing all the while,
There's only one woman's fate involved.

I reach for Family,
The concept
So maybe I'll have something
I've never really had before
That time away helped me learn and grow
And *yearn*...

It would be so much better
If we did this together,
Weaving a tapestry
Of family life, in vibrant colors...
Instead of this one sticky web life,
Entangling, drawing in mine.

Puppet strings to fulfill a need?
Imprisoning wire at ankles and feet?
Or merely a garrote, left loose...
A subtext of
More me, more hands and feet to use.

I used to escape those threads
And I have now returned.

—Monday 1 February 2021

Don't Lie

Rosemary taught me
Honesty
Caring for her mother.

To honor the frail 102 year old bones
You don't lie.

A nurse tech heard her say,
"I'm hungry," wanting the breakfast
She'd just had, before we helped give her a shower.
The tech lied, and said, "We'll give it to you."

It's so simple a thing.
Between breakfast and lunch.
But I could hear the endless lies
Threaded in those words...
It's easier to pretend, to lie
To those who cannot remember.
And Rosemary taught me
Honesty. I said, instead,
When confronted just the same:
"We just had breakfast...
We're going to do lunch soon."

This is what is happening.
It is not Dorothy who died aged 103.
My mother, who is slowly getting confused.

I will make memory easy.
I will not lie.

—Monday 15 February 2021

Dementia

Demens, dement-
The Latin...
Out of one's mind
Going mad,
Going nuts.
The scary word: Insane.

My mother
Does not want to be seen
As crazy.

The outer meaning,
The outer world
Judging such a term...

And yes,
I can see:
She is losing her mind.
The madness of it,
The sense of lunacy
With the sundowning
Deranging
Her stories,
Her thoughts,
Her very memories.

I can no longer
Hear the word
Demented as a joke,
“You’re so demented!”
A wicked, gleeful impish
Wild and weird choice.

There is no choosing here.
Demens, dement-
The Latin
For a terrible
Capricious aging.

—Monday 8 March 2021

Will it be raw?

"Will it be raw?"
She asks after I've talked
About lamb I want to cook.
I wonder why she would think
I'd serve her raw meat.

She's been so engaged,
I forgot that this is...
Still part of it,
The flared insult of dementia
Going two ways.

"Sometimes people eat raw meat,"
She explains when I can't help
But explore the why—
Stung, hurt, insulted by her question.
"That's sushi," I reply.
It is one of her favorite meals.

I never asked, "Will it be raw,"
This wounding sometimes sharp,
Sometimes soft upon my proud skin...
Revealing what aging is doing
To my mother's mind.

I am the one who must remember
That it is not my mother
Who would ask these questions,
And accept, deflect,
Struggle with the offence
To her mind, as well as mine.

"Will it be raw?"
Yes. My heart
Like tenderized meat,
With stranger questions than this.

—Monday 8 March 2021

The Good, and...

I cannot deny
There has been a great deal
Of laughter. The silliest things
Can set us off.
We can no longer be serious
When doing kickback PT exercises.
I had said, "It reminds me of a cat,
In a cat box."
Or some silly face,
Comedic timing of a pause.

We laugh a lot.

It is the daily grief
That catches me off guard.
The death of her memories,
Piece by piece,
Or some small piece
Of logical normal thinking.
So I laugh with her,
And as she does not notice
The slow loss
Of her own mind...

I weep alone.

—Monday 8 March 2021

Cherry Blossoms on the Wind

The carpet of cherry blossom
Petals upon my couch,
The floor, and path leading to the lower garden.
I breathe in the scent of refuge
Amid the mournful calls of the owl
Saying night is over.
The croak of the frogs hails the morning
Amid the beginning surge of song
From waking birds my mother never seems to hear.

These things are so bright
The owls' hoots glowing like a full moon
And the garden a celebration of sun,
Even under the gloom of rain clouds.

They are as insubstantial as my breath
This scent of spring, a haze around me
Thick as pollen, yet hard to reach.
I cannot gather it all to me, and my mother never sees.
Refuge, a pause, listening to the sounds
Of life around us, feeling the petals
Drop upon my skin, under my feet
With the fading night and liminal day.

She will look upon the garden,
From her window from her chair,
And tell me there are no more birds in the yard.
I carry the burdens of her aging as new life bursts forth
From a garden I planted that she can see
From the anchor of her routine,
The first new flowers in her garden, in years.
She will only sit there and see,
And will not rise and greet these new blossoms.
I can breathe in this transitional time
For a moment when it is not light, not night,
And she has not yet risen from her bed,
To gather up petals fallen in spring with bird song,
And toss them into the dawning wind,
To mark a threshold of transitory time and life.
For there is a carpet of cherry blossoms
Upon my patio's couch, and upon the path to the garden.

—Saturday 10 April 2021

The Garden Cannot Compare.

Please don't forget me
While I live in this
Dusking cave of my
Mother's life.
The shadows grow thick
Around us here.
They hold me, pretending
To be you, my friends.
I cannot always call upon you
Here in this darkening life,
Where the flowers
I planted for her
Are among the only bright lights,
With her rising laughter
And growing joy in them.
Yet their colored constancy
Is dim compared to the few
Moments shared with you,
My friends.
Please don't forget me.

—Friday 9 April 2021

Cathedral Colors

I escape my mother's home
To investigate the planned paths
That are now along ones
We used to forge and explore as children.
There is even parking.

There are cathedral colors
Shining through the unglazed windows
Of the old pump tower...
Gloom and light through bare metal window frames
And the open doorway.

We used to play here,
Forging through the underbrush,
Following the creek.
It was lonely, then, I'm sure,
Without this paved road
On the other side of the creek.
In the gloom of this old edifice
Light comes and reveals colors
As vibrant as cathedral glass,
Layers and layers of graffiti,
Mostly of joy, it seems to me with colors this rich
Yet I am still saddened by this old stone
Given this strange new life,

Unintended: Bright colors, and cuss words
Amid symbols of peace,
My childhood memories taken over
By time and the capricious use of spray paint.

I return to my mother's home again
Remembering the weight of wet carpet, and the stench of mold,
Layers of moss and grime upon the deck.
The concrete now patched, and sealed, deck now cleaned.

I return to the colors of the garden
Now finally tended,
And the vague image of my mother
Waving at me from her glazed window.

—Wednesday 21 April 2021

Begonia

I hear the wheels of her walker
Upstairs, rolling over hidden tension.
Is she going to be mad
That I didn't put
The begonia where she wanted?
Can she tell that I did not water it?
Like lines of her movement etched in carpet
Are lines over my long buried fears.
My shoulder ache from the effort
Of moving a potted plant to where
I will see it washing our dishes.
Or are they tight from waiting for
Her anger as I wonder: Why am I here?

—Monday 5 July 2021

Addendum:

Except I know why:
She cannot live alone,
Like that potted plant,
Which withers when neglected.

Part Two

Secret Slap

I am considered
Compassionate by some
Yet I flinch when
My mother thanks me
When I perform a simple task
Or she strokes my hair
When I am kneel
To put medication
On her arthritic knees.

Each time I help her
She is reminded:
She is helpless
She needs care
She took me away from my life.

Her thanks is gloved
By this hidden shame
And a frightening
Soul shattering helplessness.

This gratitude comes
With a secret slap
That stings both our cheeks
Despite the giving
And receiving of Loving Care.

—Saturday 1 April 2023

A Moment of Prose: Fall Risk

For the first time in weeks, I put night cream on my face before bed.

A tiny thing, one of the smallest in my self-care toolbox, and ought to be routine. My meditation pillow remains neglected. Routine comes and goes.

I'd had a year where Mom was stronger. I wrote two rough draft novels. I started to learn Chinese, because 不为什么 (bú wèi shén-me): Why not? My mind, as when at my own home: always ready for more.

So many self-care tools scattered in my space. Phrases, terms slowly delineating between comfort foods, and numbing foods.

Comfort foods comfort me, celebrate and nurture my body in healthy ways, like walks in nature.

Numbing foods: a sign, an alert that I'm hitting my limit.

Scotch, chocolate, potato chips, and binge watching "stupid TV". No amount of positive talk, meditating, or tea is enough, and 18 hours off a week *doesn't* cut it.

My sister can no longer come down every six weeks to give me my 'week of weekends' off to visit my own home.

Being on call—just a little less on call when the paid

caregivers come—is relentless. Writing, walking, much less learning new languages: forgotten.

My internal resources—reading, learning, creating art or novels—often have to go on pause. Those moments of life carry me, even when I feel empty. Even when I am exhausted and cannot pick up a tool of self-care. They are the spark at the back of me that I don't see still lighting my way.

I had a year of almost normal.

My time almost felt mine; I did things for myself.

And then she somehow slid out of her chair. That chair I hate so much. That chair she loves because it turns, and she can rock back to nap—and rock forward to get out of her chair, into the arms of her walker, spilling her out in a precarious move that puts all her caregivers on edge. It's not the walking that risks a fall, of late, but that damned chair.

And after years, somehow, strangely... she slid out of it during a caregiver's watch. When I got there, she was beet red, tension so high, there was no point in checking her BP. I tried to get her to lay down in her bedroom, but she refused. "There's nothing to see there."

That painful statement: It's why a stable easy chair is something she'd refuse, even one that would help her stand. Why that damned padded, easy chair rocking thing is so important to her.

This slip was followed by a weekend of vertigo when she'd turn in the night, or sit up.

A year of testing out my self-care toolkit...

With now 18 hours of Visiting Angels...

And so... here we go.

To the renewed confusion, that now seems never gone.

The "Fake Butter" Tub

I'll admit...
I judge the way she
Stabs into a tub
Of margarine.
I see the deep gouge
And wonder:
Was that aimed at me?
Her having to be here
To care for our Mom
To give me a break so I can go home?
It seems a sign of anger–
But my interpretation
Is only an echo of mine.
I scrape the top of the contents...
So politely.
Daily making Mom's
Cheese and crackers,
Nutella sandwiches, or grilled cheese.
My own frustrations revealed
In the quirk of a wrist,
The scoop of a knife,
The gouge I translate with
My own feelings and fears.
How much I...
Too often...
Don't want to be here.

How much...
I know...
I still must, daily,
Put "fake butter" on
Mom's meals.

—Friday 3 February 2023

Home or Home

I had the last of the wine I bought
On a day trip up home.
The taste of the tempranillo
Reminds me of my friend's laughter—
The man who made it—
Talking with my second daughter,
The hug of another friend,
And the tubes of gouache waiting for me in my car...
Feeling at home, myself...
I remember that now, knowing when I opened the bottle
I wouldn't be able to stay.

But I am drinking at my mother's home.
The earthy taste of my friend's wine,
Reminding me that one can never go back
To one's childhood home again... Not really.

But I'll remember the laughter
As I finish the wine, and hope to get paint on my hands
And that the earthy feel of the gouache
Will then remind me of the tempranillo...

And home.

—Thursday 23 February 2023

My Covered Patio I

The storm came
When I needed it.
I could have had a call
With my lover
But I was irritated.
A shower only made
Me want to cry,
But, as ever, no tears came.

And then I heard the thunder
And went outside to read,
Drink scotch,
And to hear hail hit the ground
In a random rhythm
Against growling clouds
And dazzled night
Flaring in staccato beats
With the rain and ice.

Even if she rings the bell
I let the storm be me,
Let it speak my feelings
Under solar string of lights
now lit in the night.

—Sunday 26 March 2023

My Covered Patio II

Will I hear the call bell?
With a storm
Stoppering my ears
With pressure and sound?

I don't know.
But the storm rails and screams
And weeps for me,
In the one pocket of the night
I rarely get to use.

I listen to the storm,
And count after light till
The spectacle of sound:
How far away is the storm?
But a count of three...
Is that in miles?

Technically I'm still on duty
I always am. Not just a dutiful child
But a caregiver, someone
Who will take care of needs
Even in the middle of the night.

But the rain surrounding
My patio
On three sides
Gives me a sense of freedom

—Sunday 26 March 2023

My Covered Patio III

Lightning strikes
With a thunderclap
That seems to go through
My covered patio.
I'm loving it here.
Protected from
the rain
the lightning
the storm
the ding of the bell.

It is night.
And Mom should be asleep
But what does that matter
When she wakes
Several times in the night

She doesn't always need me.

As a child
She was always terrified of storms.
Because I'm here
She feels safe
But I'm not sure if I can hear her call me.
The alarm bell that I set up
Will it carry over the sound of rain?

If there was no thunder
If there was no lightning
Was no hail
I might be dancing
Out in the backyard
Pretending
I was a nature goddess
Or maybe just a witch
Someone free to enjoy nature
Not just on a porch or a patio.

Not someone always alert
To hear the sound a call bell
Over the sound of the rain.

—Sunday 26 March 2023

My Covered Patio IV

A train...
We forget that a train track
Was laid nearby.
I think we rarely hear it.
But why do I hear it in the storm?
The call bell, the whistle
That loud alert
And then the sound
Of the wheels on the track
Only stopped by the loudest crack
Of thunder...
And then the flooded creek
Seems to take over
The sound of the train

A daily occurrence
A life, perhaps,
Taken over by the storm

—Sunday 27 March 2023

My Covered Patio V

But here I have
A book
A scotch
Stolen time

The huge carafe of water
I drink as well
The tears unshed

The sense of guilt
For feeling
Any of this
The need
To be alone.

—Sunday 27 March 2023

Endless Question

I can eat healthy.
I can take herbs and adaptogens
That deal with stress.
I have caregivers three afternoons a week.
Eighteen precious hours.

I mowed
I did yard work
I sweated...
I got dizzy because
I was working that hard...
Even the expenditure
Of physical exercise isn't enough.
To balance against the stress...

But the endless question...
Why isn't love enough?

—Thursday 30 March 2023

I'm Not a Parent Again

They say it's like parenting again.
It's not.
From a baby to an adult
There's this never-ending joy
Of watching my children
Experience discovery—good or bad.
I would protect them from harm or death

Now, I can do little protecting.
I can only watch the slow march towards the tomb.
My mother content to only sit in her chair.

When I prepared my daughters
For their independence...
Age deprives my mother of hers.
I take it into my hands
And hope I don't mess it up
Because there will be
No growing out of my mistakes.

Once, my mistakes could only
Help my daughters grow.

Now? The cost of messing up?
My mom's care, and the quality of life that she has left.

Parents watch their children rise into life
A caregiver watches their parents descend into their death,
And there is absolutely no comparison
And there is absolutely no changing that
No more challenges and hope
We only open the door and step further into grief.

—Some time in January 2023

Addendum : Still Not a Parent Again

Parents can take
A baby's ankles in one hand,
Lift to wipe their bottom clean.
Impossible to do the same
With a bedridden adult.

—Sunday 2 March 2025

Pee... All About Pee

She would hang support panties
On the doorknob
Of her bathroom
To reuse.

Fearing UTIs not only for infection but the added evil:
Subsequent signs of apparent dementia.

We talked about it. She stopped hanging them up.
When her knees groaned, she finally agreed to a bedside potty...

On a Monday she has an accident
With pee down her legs
And on the floor... My own feet wet
As I care and clean, and change the potty.

Another Monday another accident.
"It's dry!" she claims. "You don't believe me?"
She asks, accusing me, angrily, defensively.
"Mom, they're made that way. To feel dry."

I'm astonished that we argue. The argument goes on.
I decide to show her my point. We experiment.
The Depend can take at least FOUR CUPS...
Even if it feels dry, when does it start to spill over?

And then the question: How long has she been wearing them?
It's hard to voice my fear.

Night Time Ones have blue.
"It looks plastic."
I assure her. "That's to help you feel dry."
We discuss when to wear them.
"I'm too tired. I'll try them tomorrow."
And: "I tried them before. They itch."
This is untrue; and it's painful
To remind her she's never had them.
Just like she's said, about my menstrual cups,
"I know what that's like; I've used them."
She had a hysterectomy before they were made.
From her description she's thinking of pads.

"They're clean. I wear a tissue between the legs."
I say nothing about the tissue, as there's no point.
It's routine. They're worn a bit higher.
I know she does it to feel clean.
"Mom, that doesn't mean it hasn't been used."

"If I wear them do I wear them the next day?"
I have to tell her "No, mother." Night time for night, the others for day.

Only to discover
The Next Night, at bedtime, she must have forgotten.
She had worn it all night, and all day, and expected to wear them...
Again... Still...
That night. I remind her again.

What I hate is the fight.
Caught off guard, I can't help but be shocked, to feel angry, to feel scared.
Will I have to remind her again? Why is this so hard?
"No, Mom, this is how you do this? Did you wear
The same underwear
All the time?"

Underwear, using the toilet, even like pads... like women do for years...
How is this new? How is it so hard to understand? Why is it a fight?
Heartbreaking.
And one sister doesn't want to hear it. She hears it too much at work.
(I confess I cross that boundary, talking about the pee).
The other one, I'd have to copy Mom on an email... and
I promised Mom not to point out these things to her... Unless she asks.

(So I don't write that sister, because I won't rub it in Mom's face
That... well...) It's something to point to.
This... This is THAT.
That thing we're afraid of, that we don't want to confront.
And it's leaking around the edges
Like Mom's pee in a support panty, a Depend worn too long
Because it feels dry.

So it's not about pee, and not only about pee...

But pee, and panties, support or otherwise, Depends, and such...
And I want to cry. I feel so alone. I can't argue with her...
I can't but try...
To clean up the pee when she has another accident.
And everything leaks around the edges.

—Thursday 6 April 2023

Ten Minutes Away

Her appointment
Is just ten minutes away.
Scheduling 45 minutes
To get out the door...
We'll hopefully
Be on time.

—Tuesday 4 April 2023

Family Stories and Memories

I sometimes think that when I die
You'll still be
The keeper of the stories.
You know so much
Of the family history
My trauma erased.
When we laughed tonight
Over something silly,
Three sisters—and Mom trying
To keep up, and we three
Threading her back...

In our laughter
While we reminisced,
And you told stories.
Your eyes sparkled.

I loved it. It was like starlight.
Nighttime and birdsong.
I wondered if, when I'm old,
When I might be dying,
If you'd tell me the stories again.
All the things that held us together,

Giving me back a childhood
That I forgot in my trauma...

But we can never cross
That bridge again from
Our childhood, my trauma,
The fractures of your pain,
As Mom's memories fade,
And our fractured sisterhood
Yawns deeper and more distant…
My lost memories will die with her,
Keeping one treasured memory of your laugh,
When it seemed you forgot
To be angry with me.

—Sunday 4 March 2023, Saturday 8 April 2023

Fundamental Errors

I quote *Gaudy Night*
All the time.
The book you gave me.
Tonight I watched you laugh...
And we, oh my heart...
Laughed together.
I hadn't thought it possible.
The rift between us—
I don't know if you know—
I did moderate my behavior.
You did make me think.
But I know we both hadn't
Made merely surface errors.
The deepest scars I gave you,
Though,
Are as familiar as my own.
The ones you gave me
So deep they still bleed.

When caregiving our mother,
I cannot afford to lose so much heart.
The hows and whys
Would probably echo
Each other's.

After you left,
After the sparkle of your laughter faded
I wondered
If we'd love again,
Because some wounds
Some pain, even so fundamental
Echo our quoting in counterpoint,
From Sayers' *Gaudy Night*.

—Saturday 4 March 2023

Names of Neighbors

She tells me the names,
Of neighbors out on their walk
And that of the dogs,
Goodness and Beth.
Their daughter, Mom tells me,
"They call her Mer."

This is something I told her,
Two years ago, because she does not get out.
I spoke to them while gardening,
And giving treats to the pets.
Does she tell me
To remind herself?
To assure both me and herself
That she hasn't forgotten?
Does she tell me now,
Because it's somehow new?

I do not know.

—Sunday 5 March 2023

Mom's Knees

Mom's knees
Sounded like branches breaking.
When I held her hips
To help her when she tried
To simply sit
I could feel the vibrations
Of the sound of her pain
In my fingertips.

—Thursday 16 March 2023

Caregiver: Overwhelmed.

I have not showered
For three days,
Nor changed clothes for two
And I'm not sure
That I'd call it depression.
When knees that groaned
Like branches waiting to break,
I'd wake to the call bell,
To walk with
My mother, the owner of
Those arthritic knees,
So she can safely pee in the night.

And also... bills, both hers and mine
Chores and laundry
Meds to manage...
Calming stress,
Trying to diminish pain...

While my tears are held back
Beyond my eyes
Damned up by the tension
In my shoulders...
I'd still not use the word: depression.
I can only say
Caregiver: Overwhelmed.

—Monday 20 March 2023

A Loss that Predeceased Her

You hugged me
With all the show of warmth.

My apologies.
I misunderstood.
Hope had intervened.
You apparently...
Didn't mean it.

But then, perhaps...
I never knew you.
There are too many
Fundamental Errors
To be friends again,
Much less loving sisters.

So it becomes not only
The slow care and waiting
Dread of the death
Of our dear mother,
It is the end of the fracturing
Of her family that predeceases her.

If you were to embrace me again
Eyes lit like a friend's,
I will embrace you
As if I embrace the dead.
And mourn in private.

—Monday 20 March 2023

Set Aside for a Sunday

A friend
Dismissed it as normal.
"I grew up
Seeing that in church."
All those false hugs,
False smiles,
Where hate was
Put aside for a Sunday.
I said,
"But they knew all the rules."
And I had not,
When you hugged me.
Your eyes alight
With what I thought
Was warmth.
My hope buried
Like a puppy's bone
Come out,
And I bounced around
So happy.

And then I was told
Not to read into that.
And, “It’s not about you.”

But hugs and smiles
And shared laughter
Should be
About me, about you...
About us,
In family.
Especially a caregiving one.
But it was hatred
Set aside for a day
Like a Sunday.
And I never knew.

—Monday 20 March 2023

Caregiving Opens Unhealed Wounds.

She'd been reading a book
On love, family, affection.
And asked me if I'd felt the
Five, but actually six,
Requirements of a healthy family.
I said… "No. You weren't alone."
Love and affection?
To look at us now—
Fractured bonds, and more.
Two years prior both sisters had said:
"I'm doing this for you…"
For Me…Not our mother,
When coming to help me give care.
The unhealed wounds
Of a fracture four years old,
Fracturing even wider in the years that came.
"No, there was love," I tell her,
"But not enough."
And I think, I must practice
The Art of Letting Go.

—Monday 20 March 2023

Somehow, I Still Love My Sister

The bonds had been fractured
Before our mother broke her hip.
She came to help, dropped everything,
But her wounds, our wounds unhealed.

Then Mom fell again, and then again
In the space of thirty days, one year later,
And a miserable Thanksgiving.
And I erred, applying the balm of an ill mother
Over all that pain and wounding still unhealed.

Trying to be a family, and care give together...
We only ripped our wounds wider.
And now I think they will never heal
Because I hoped we'd bond over care.

—Wednesday 22 March 2023

I Forgot My Mantra

Mom was home, with a new hip joint
And I would run a string of knots
Through my fingers with a mantra of
"Don't fix. Don't fix. Don't fix..."
When watching either of my sisters
Speak with Mom, and my the thread of knots
Helping me see the tripwires grow
Between them, hopelessly tangled.

"Don't fix. Don't fix. Don't fix..."
I should have remembered, because now
I'm caught in the tripwires I helped make
Caught, entangled, and it's too late
For a mantra, and a knotted string
To save a family with too much going on

Because I tried to fix it, and I failed.

—Wednesday 22 March 2023

HOME and...

I love my mother.
I love my family.

But I wonder at the terms.
Are they a cultural construct?

Mom's friends seem
So amazed by my care.

I feel the grating edge
Of family obligation.

Not only in loving care,
But discordant sisterhood.

There are days love
Feels like a pretense.

I came here on a lie.
Not mine. But hers.

She could have hired
Caregivers... at any time

Years before we
Established my obligations.

I love my family.
I love my mother.

Exile

I am still
In Exile.
This home
Is not my Home.

At least...

My daughters
Thrive

In the home
We built.

—Sunday 26 March 2023

Alice's Baby

I've lost count of the times we've had conversations like this. Friends, caregivers and my sisters never seem to have them. I'm left alone to respond to something like this, that comes so randomly.

"What do you want to watch tonight," I ask.
She chooses Vicar of Dibley.
"I want to know about the baby."
"Oh?" I ask. A safe reply: *Oh?* When I'm caught off guard.
"I wonder how it works..."
I can only commiserate. "How what works?"
"Having the baby in front of all those children!"
And she is *angered*, and I am more startled.
The night before we watched the show, when Alice gave birth,
The baby supposedly born in a barn during a Christmas festival.
"How could they do that?" she says, offended.
I take a deep breath and rally to respond.
Carefully challenging her confusion, I say, "You know it's fake, right?"
Her face changes, braving humiliation, she asks. "You must think I'm stupid."
I breathe again, and try for a good reply.
Hoping not to hurt her, I say, "Charmingly Childlike."

At least she laughs, and we're back on some safe—if still shifting—ground.
These conversations are more frequent.
I could write a list of these things, and chart their frequency each time they happen.
I hear the echo of Mom's angered defense, "You don't believe me?"
And these moments of her cognitive confusion...
Are not ones I can point to.
For so many it's not these conversations that matter—
They don't impact her daily life,
They just leak around the edge of her aging,
Leaving me alone to respond, rescuing the rending of her reality.

—Saturday 8 April 2023

Anyway, but FAR More...

Make breakfast, lunch, dinner
Prepare for the next day.
Celebrate she can
Make her own bed—most days
My own room's a mess.

It hurts like a headache
That daily life looks
So simple.
Things I'd do *anyway*,
If not on my schedule,
But the space between chores
Have become so damned heavy.

Her breathing when she goes
From room to room
Is like she's on the last leg of a marathon,
And her confusion
Makes my own heart race,
And the words adding weight
To the barbell.

Make coffee, breakfast...
Prepare for the next day
Try to remember my own room,
To make my own bed.

Carrying these caregiving duties,
A workout that adds the pounds,
And it feels insane,
That it's all for chores
I'd still be doing *anyway!*

—Saturday 8 April 2023

Two Years... After the Falls

The door closed
Upon the tomb,
Scraping on my fingers.
My fears realized.
I do wait upon a living death.
Her inertia subdues
My creativity, at times,
Like a resurrection defier.

My friends...
I rarely see them now.
The few phone calls
The few moments of creativity
Are like me pulling the string
On the burial bells,
Saying:
"I'm still alive!"

—Saturday 8 April 2023

Listen...

My father used to say,
"Music must be listened to,"
When I'd fret about sounds
So soft they were
Like whispers
Or bass notes felt, not heard.
Right now, I can't tell
If I'm the violin or the string...
Waiting for the pluck and pull
Of the discordant notes of my mother's life.
The pause in this strange symphony
Leaves me tense and waiting
For that next note
Which might tell me of changes
She cannot share... or does not—
Like the lump in her breast
She said not a word about for three months—
I track these things in her confusion
That rises from her anxiety.

I do not know the melody,
And question the counterpoinnt.
It leaves me nothing to point to
As I hear something wrong in the way
She tracks her old stories,

Comments on long dead actors,
Wondering if they're still alive,
Confusion about the reality of TV shows…
Nothing to point to,
Nothing for a doctor to diagnose
And give a pill for.

I can only say I listen
For the drumbeat upon the floor
Of a fall that doesn't happen,
Except that I'm listening
For some other mysterious music
That might finally come for my sisters
And me, of her final symphony.

—Friday 21 April 2023

Listen II...

Doctors—and others—
Like melodies,
Sound bites that let them
Recognize the well known symphonies
By only the well known overtures.

I can't blame them.

They're not families who listen
To the arduous hours of how
A particular symphony is composed.
Our own concert hall
Where strange, discordant notes
Are practiced upon our inexperienced ears.
We think they're supposed to understand,
To make for us this music pretty and peaceful
For all the world to hear
Her life was so beautiful, but not...
The strange music of capricious aging.

—Friday 21 April 2023

Listen III...

I think:
Why don't you hear it?
For me this is all as loud as a scream
A discordant off note
In an otherwise beautiful song.
I can't tell if I'm the violin box,
Or just the ready string
Tense and waiting to be plucked
Vibrating in this music
I hopefully won't break
In the confusing,
Unfamiliar rhythms.

—Friday 21 April 2023

It's Like Caught Gears Or...

My father had two old record players.
He had such refined needles.
We played with the old one.
Sometimes vinyl will skip.

I tell her about a visit
I will make on my time off,
Visiting a friend and their rescue dog.
"He lives there..."
She says, trying to place him,
Pointing to his old house.

He hasn't lived there in 30 years.
Sold the house for his mother in the last two.

The needle skipping over memories,
Stuttering, starting, trying to find
The reality, the groove, the song...

And it happens more and more, lately.
Daily now.

—Friday 21 April 2023

Her Friends...

Her friends
Are starting to see it now.

It's rare that she sees them.
They come to celebrate birthdays
Every few months.
Mom is content in her chair,
Staring out the window... napping...
Thinking of stories she no longer
Will sit down and write.
Sleeping.

The effort of company,
Even beloved friends.
Is exhausting.

—Friday 21 April 2023

Putting on Socks

The effort
Of being old
Makes her breathe
As if she's at the end
Of an endurance race.
In the effort of putting on
Her house gown,
And pulling on socks...
She has to pause
And catch her breath
For each foot
Of this... race.

—Sunday 23 April 2023

You can buy them online

The stressors were gone,
Her confusion remained.
She's tired more...
Is it a UTI
That insidious, possible cause?
Easily fixed?
She refuses to go to the doctor
For something she can't see
Or feel.
I realize now...
One day...
I might have to fight her on this.
But for now:
UTI test strips can be bought
Online.

—Wednesday 26 April 2023

The start of it all

A friend's mother broke her leg,
Causing all the fuss of caregiving and more.
Her confusion grew
And the doctors started using words
Like hospice, and the end, and Alzheimer's.
Till they finally caught the cause of it all: a UTI.
Had it slowed her reaction time?
Was her confusion so great that she hit the wrong pedal
In her car that day?
Within days of antibiotics...
Her mind was clear.

I wept when my own mother's test strip
Said her urine was clean.

—Wednesday 26 April 2023

Two True Stories

One:
His wife told me
About his alcoholism.
His aggression,
And his slow decline.
I'm sure the beer didn't help
His Alzheimer's.
He'd forget he'd been drinking,
So much he'd pass out,
Wake, and start drinking again...
Till she finally got him into
A facility.
And there was no one left–
Except me, who bought her groceries
And the very few friends she had left–
To witness her own decline
Hoarding cats that must have smelled
Worse than the vomit and beer.

Two:
Her grandson
Told me of how his father
Struggled with his mother's
Dementia, and that she smoked
And would forget...
And risk burning down
The family home.
Till one day, she forgot she smoked.
And asked,
"Why are all these lighters everywhere?"
And he replied they were for candles
In case the power went out.
She never smoked again.

I watch my own mother's
Battle, and pray that the stories
I will tell, will never be as violent
Or as humorous, even if...
Just as painful.

—Thursday 27 April 2023

Part Three

How Are You?

She wanted
To use
Clorox Wipes
On her bottom
During her shower.

Why am I
So caught off guard
Even with expectation?
Shared reality
Or shared common sense...
Gone.

—Wednesday 24 May 2023

A Moment of Prose: Who do I want to be?

I asked myself a question when entering perimenopause. "Who do I want to be on the other side of this?" I asked myself that same question on the last Tuesday in July. And answered, "Someone who copes with stress."

In a flash I realized that I pictured myself free from stress with all the coping. Almost three years in, *shouldn't I be good at this*? I couldn't tell if my sense of exhaustion was menopausal, or a physiological coping when all other self-care tools were exhausted.

The changes I see in my mother feel microcosmic, and yet it feels as if the path took a sharp left in May.

The sing-songs she now does when we work on a puzzle together, so odd, so childlike, sometimes like a nah-nahnny-boo-boo taunt with teasing about all the puzzle pieces she wants to find being in my half of the box. There is almost too much anger for this sing-song taunt to be cheerful.

And then we talk. She asks me questions.

The girl who clicked her heels and flew, her name was Dorothy, right?

And ducks and swans are not alike, right?

To the last: How are they different, Mom? I reply, learning some strange variant of patience.

She demonstrates, and I wonder if the words are gone, that ducks are smaller, and swans puffier—her mouth poofed out, her arms out. I ask about necks, and she lifts her head, and says that swans necks are bigger. Longer, I say.

And ducks don't fly.

Yes, they do, Mom.

The pain in her knees is so bad she cannot stand up straight. When walking, there are times she can't even lift her head, looking down at this torturous path between the wheels of her walker, from her chair to her bathroom and thence to bed.

And writing it all down, it's seeable by anyone, but daily they're often only five-minute exchanges in a thirty-six-hour day, even the helpless witnessing of her pain—knowing there's nothing I can do.

Despite having Olay cleansing cloths, and misplaced vaginal wipes, she somehow still hunted down the Clorox wipes, and then asked me if we could use them for her shower.

A long moment of one deep breath, and that painful, protective and defensive patience, I said, "No; why not a washcloth?"

She refused, somehow fixated on the Clorox wipes idea. Her first request was for something far better for her bottom than those harsh chemicals—and I had accepted that, so was more caught off guard with the display of such serious lack of caution.

It was as if we'd turned some strange corner of this once familiar house.

And there was no turning back.

And I knew that I must give myself, and her, plenty of grace.

During this time, I listened to a Huberman Labs episode with Elisa Epple. I read her book. I'm no longer astonished that those who deal with chronic caregiving stress take nine days longer to heal from a wound. The stress gets into our very cells, with this desperate desire to stop all this impossible-to-stop from actually happening, to try and protect our loved ones from going through more pain, more confusion—the stress of knowing this is impossible.

There is no art in letting go.

It is difficult to embrace uncertainty, when uncertainty is often not merely uncertain, but strange, and painful, and another layer of grief.

I hid away the Clorox wipes and knew that this was one thing I had witnessed where her mind might have impacted her daily life. And this was that thing we'd all so desperately never wanted to watch happen.

It was here.

Two months of realizing that this was a stress that not all the tools in the box will help fade into peace. The tools can only help carry it with a sense of love, which is the only possible way to get through. And even that is not enough.

A List of Ten

There are ten things
To look for
In our elder's life
To know that dementia
Has taken their minds...
Too bad this aging
Doesn't always follow
The rules,
Allowing it all to fold
In on itself,
Like my mother's stories

They say this list
Is what lies ahead, but not...
To read it this way.
But I did, and it caused me pain.
Two and a half years,
I could see such subtle signs...
Feeling alone in this,
Wishing I could stem the tide,
Put my finger in the dam.
I, the only one who witnessed
This daily.
The MOCA scores, putting her
Upon the edge of all this now...

—Thursday 6 July 2023

Saturday 30 April 2023

1. Memory Disrupts Daily Life

The stories don't matter
Where they fold and unfold
Upon each other.
People, places, times merging
Into others.
Those folded, unfolding memories
Don't matter.
It doesn't disrupt her life.
It only disturbs me—and her...
Till she forgets.

2. Challenges in Problem Solving

I took over the bills
Before they went awry.
One missed bill
The check written
But gone, never arrived.
She's confused over bills now,
And I cannot get the caregivers
To not give her mail.
She's distressed.
She's not in control,
And she's unsafe in this confusion.
But what happenned to that lost check?
We will never known.

3. Difficulty completing a familiar task.

She forgot how to attach
A document to an email—
The former queen of Inter-Library-Loan.
Does this count as memory
Disrupting daily life?
A lost piece in a routine?
A task done thousands of times?
Till the memory unfolded itself,
That wrinkled fabric of thinking,
After I showed her, and helped her
A number of times.

4. Confusion with Time or Place

The blessed routine!
She began it on her own,
But I defend it, protect it—
The hedge against sundowners.
I only see confusion in her stories, for now,
When she recollects
The past, retells stories she's written,
And cities and countries,
People and places
Merge into one another
Like crumpled linen.
The routine prevents her
From getting lost in her own house.

I hope.

5. Trouble understanding visual images

A pink poster, across the street,
With a child's fondness of glitter and glue
Like the stars of the Milky Way arching over
A child's drawing of a Unicorn.
I had to describe the picture,
For she could not see it, despite binoculars.
But she did not know what unicorns were,
Even when I described them.
Three times she pointed at the griffins
On a small cabinet, "Like those?"
No, mother, horses with a horn.
She let go of her distress, and decided
This poster must be for a birthday party,
Her mind has decided, and declared this,
Stating that Unicorns are November's Zodiac.

Long gone are the days when she introduced
Her three daughters to books about zodiacs
Thick with descriptions on these sun signs.
And despite this painful moment—
Unicorns are far more fun than scorpions.

6. Problems with words, speaking and writing.

Finding the right words, the book says
"Party people" instead of "newlyweds."
She has done this now, several times
Hiccups in her thoughts, I barely register now.

She still reads, rereads endlessly, her own
Written stories, and edits them sharply.

7. Misplacing Things

Her files... strewn over her desk
A wild compilation of years and subject
Letters mixed with bills
A perfect example
Of the wrinkles and folds of her mind.

8. Displaying Poor Judgement

See the poems about Pee... All about Pee
That is still a problem, shifting and changing
Something I will no doubt revisit
As her mobility and thinking change over...
I would have said months, or weeks...
I'm in terror that it might be days.

9. Withdrawing from Social Activities

This has gone on for so long
It is part of her daily life long before
My twin cared for her, taking her shopping
Once a week. Long before I took over
These minimal caregiving duties,
Long before I moved in.
Only twice has she said,
"That was a good meeting,"

When the Birthday Girls—Faculty Wives—
Came together, or even when
Her beloved writers group had met.
The anticipation of exhaustion even before
Any festivities started.

10. Changes in Mood and Personality

Her defensive, "You don't believe me?"
Tells me a part of her knows what's happening.
Even as I protect her comfort zone
The danger is from within,
And my unfortunate confrontation
With my own fear and pain,
Makes me the author of my own doubts.

Her Sing Song

We've done puzzles before—
Gifts from a granddaughter,
But never before
Did she raise her feelings in
Sing song.
It is odd.
And then comes worse:
Sometimes it is a taunting song
Cheerfully malicious,
Cheerfully strange,
About puzzle pieces
That she wants, that will be found
Only in my half of the box.

She wants to entertain me.
She wants me to laugh.
When I don't, she claims
I do a "witch laugh" better
Than she, her sing song echoing
Those gleeful witchy tones.
My teeth on edge, I give her the cackle,
And try not to despair
This unexpected sundowning song.

—Thursday 6 July 2023

For the Inevitable?

At first there were six,
Then eight, now twelve
Boxes of books
Read, unfinished
The clutter of my mind
I want to send away
Send home, take home,
The one place
Where I can breathe

For some reason it hurts
To look at them
Packed to make room
For the attention of care.

I had gathered them, once,
And brought them all here
To my mother's home,
A balm to my screaming mind
So I'd have more of myself here.

Taken down from shelves
Boxed away,
They clear my mind for focus,
But it feels as if I'm packing
To go home...
For the inevitable.

With no reason to point to...
Why do I feel
It will be soon? In months
Not years? Haven't I worried
About this before?
These boxes hide my heart
Give it room to beat
But protect it:
You will have HOME again.
At Mom's house: I have no room
To cry.

—Wednesday 7 June 2023

This Exile...

I didn't want to get up today
This exile has left me
With few friends
And no supportive sisters
And scarcely now,
A home to return to.
I sense that my mother
Doesn't need ME to care for her
Any cardboard cutout will do
If it can bring her breakfast,
Pour out the potty,
And rub Voltaren on her knees,
With the routine I have guarded
Holding the facsimile up.

—Saturday 24 June 2023

Lost Pieces of My Home

She says she feels guilty
For taking me from my life.
And yes. She has...
And I have had a taste of
What I lost, going home.
Eradicated from my own home
By my own daughters
The real tragedy?
The illumination that my life
Didn't include her—nor me in hers.
There's a life to leave and lose,
Not one shared and cared for.
While devastated, I do know
The pieces of my life, my home
Can be something new, growing
Restored with the help of the two
Who brought me to this place—
Something quite foreign here!
I will accept this pain,
Knowing, hoping that I won't
Be leaving this living tomb
To return to an equally empty
Family home and life, and one better
Than the one I left—
There has to be some little reward
For all this grief and pain.

—Sunday 25 June 2023

Nine Days Longer

It takes nine days longer
For wounds to heal
In the real world proof
That ongoing, chronic stress
Of caregiving
Has costs.

I see it in my skin,
That this loving
Needs relief.

—Saturday 1 July 2023.

They All Hate It

Elizabeth told me
"They all hate it,
Even with no memory at all."
Moving, that is,
To a nursing home.

I went home.
A rare day trip—
The week of weekends
A memory six months old—
To see myself erased
By my daughters,
Replaced by a stranger,
And attacked with barking
By a surprise dog
Trying to defend
"His" territory—
My very own home!—
As I stepped inside.

This is what they must feel:
Eradicated, lost, homeless...
The landmarks of a life
Of one's own history
Consigned to a stranger,
Or a room in a basement,

A stranger sleeping
In your own bed.

A failure of my own sense
Or yearning for zen—
Where is the ME
In my mind:
A place, with things
Those subtle things that matter
Woven into a house, a home.

My refuge, my retreat gone.
Death seemed an alternative,
And my daughters worked—
Bless them, truly for understanding—
Repaired the damage.

But with gritted teeth,
And a heart that grows hard,
Or burning with anger,
When I think...
Of all those times
Someone would ask...
When I will do this
To my own mother:
Take her from her home?

—Saturday 1 July 2023

There's No Art to It

The effort of holding onto love,
The impossible, the walled off,
Rising from miscommunication
And a history of misunderstanding
Has left me with little energy—
It takes so much effort, with no reward—
For more than my mother's care.
Holding onto her life as if it were the same
Echoes of pain—the past and present
I want to fix it. I want it all better,
Let love shine light over these walls
And beyond this slow dying.

All I can do is sit, grasping onto patience
Till it becomes not love, but pain,
All the goodness squeezed out of it.
I must let go, knowing there's no art to it,
And let the impossible be just that,
And try not to change or fix immovable walls
To simply give love where it's required—
Giving loving care to a mother who needs it.

—Thursday 6 July 2023

How Bad Is It?

This morning,
Through layers of wood
Carpet, ceiling tiles,
The distance between floors,
Her room and mine,
I heard...
The now familiar sound
Of her knees,
Groaning.

They must be so bad...
I did not hear her move
From bed to bedside potty.

I know that
Even if she struggles,
When she sits in her chair,
She will be as cheerful
As she is every day.

—Thursday 13 July 2023

The Zen of Aging

Is she a Zen master
Or something
To accept all that pain
That resounds between floors
Bone upon bone
As knees try to bend
The way God intended;
Or does dementia—
Worse than imagined—
Take the memory of pain away?
But Dorothy, at 103 years of age
Had a similar thinking,
Once admitting,
After I discovered she'd
Suffered through a headache
A whole morning,
Tapping her head, she said,
"It's all in here."

I will believe
Zen Master
Like unicorns of the zodiac
For this is a more cheerful thought.

—Thursday 13 July 2023

My Own Tin Roofed Heart

He was angry,
And told his teacher
"But I'm a peaceful guy."
His teacher,
In a remote monastery
Somewhere in Thailand,
Told him,
"Go into your tin roofed hut,
Put on all your robes,
And feel your anger."

Where is all the meditation
On excising dangerous
Difficult emotions?
No, no, this teacher,
This guide, emphatically states.
Sit within all that heat.
Jack Kornfield simply
Embraces this all
As energy.

Four months away
From a three year stay,
The heat of gestating grief

And words on page
I haven't sat in this—
My own tin roofed hut,
Preferring to numb,
Distract from a meditation
Of living with
My mom's slow dying.

—Wednesday 19 July 2023

The Remaining Talismans

I'm packing away more books
And feeling my feelings.
The books left: read, unread,
Familiar, or talismanic of my past,
My writer friends, my inner journeys,
That a discerning eye would find
Ample evidence for an exegesis of me.
In what is left here, at Mom's house.
An acceptance that I must spend time
Focusing on her needs, without losing…
Without losing what makes me mine.

—Wednesday 19 July 2023

No Rose Garden

I read in a favorite old book,
I Never Promised You a Rose Garden:*
"No, no... It's the *word*
That is making you
So frightened.
It is the old evil word
[Demented]
Which once meant..."
And the word, in the book meant, once,
"Hopeless and forever."
And while one word
I fill in for another...
Mirrors the fear of my mother.
In this case...
Demens, dement-
The Latin
For a terrible
Capricious aging,
Does mean forever,
But is only hopeless,
Without love.
And I bring her flowers,
And plant them in the garden,
Begonias, impatiens, and others...
Though here, there are no roses.

—Wednesday 19 July 2023

* Joanne Greenberg, *I Never Promised You a Rose Garden.*
New York: Signet, 1964, p. 171

Pour Overs

The chocolate
Has settled in the bottom
Of my morning mocha
A treat for the next
Two days of doctor appointments.
When Mom sits
In a waiting room,
There are no books
To assuage her impatience,
My own sorrow:
We've run out of things
To say, to share.
She'll pour over her petulance
Till it will spill over
Onto me.
Like the pale taste
Of a bitter brew
But I stir the chocolate
And ready a book
And will breathe in
My own meditation of patience.

—Thursday 20 July 2023

Wait for the Waiting Room

Where did
The simple joy
Of reading go?

She's already robed me...
No... I robbed myself
By fretting about
Her inevitable petulance
In the waiting room.

But she was
An avid reader once.
Her house is filled
With books in almost every room.
Now she only reads
Her own stories, again and again,
But even that
Is no ready talisman
Against the weight
Of the waiting room.

—Thursday 20 July 2023

Why not Live...

Its just my mother.
It's the house I grew up in.
Why is it so hard?
To feel love
Swallowed up
By a lake of
Gestating grief?
Why do that?
And not just...
Live with the reverberation
Of the no doubt
Incredible pain
I can feel in my fingertips
When I help my mother
Get out of
Her new wheelchair.

—Thursday 20 July 2023

Her Mother's Mind

Anita's mother
Would call in fear.
There was a boy
In her rooms,
Of her nursing home,
Lying on the couch.
Anita—probably feeling
That bit of shock,
Becoming so familiar to me now—
Would accept surprise,
And say,
"He's probably tired.
Let him sleep."
Her mother is calmed.
Even though there was no boy.
Anita did what I
Still struggle to do:
Embrace the uncertain reality
Of her mother's mind.

—Sunday 23 July 2023

What Cannot Change

I remember Elisa Epple
Telling Huberman
About love—
Or rather...
Chronic stress:
Gripping a rope,
Attached to some
Unchanging wall.
You pull and pull and pull
Till your hands are raw—
Because you cannot
Change
Anything.

Love wants to give.
And giving joy, peace.
Love doesn't want to watch
The struggles of pain.
Sitting still
Feels like agreeing
To that invisible force
That's not so unseen—
The aged body, destroyed knees
The spirit exhausted
From carrying a body
Ten feet, and more...

Love is supposed to be
The shared time
Over puzzles,
And meals,
And TV before bed.

Love releases
What cannot change...
It must,
Or break
And gives time
Such precious tme
In joys that can—still
Be shared.

—Sunday 23 July 2023

Part Four

Hold Both

Love...
You hold both
Agony and Joy
In your hands,
And do not shy away.
Grief might wait
At the door.
But birds come to the feeders
By the windows
Amid the garden flowers
Planted for happiness

—Sunday 23 July 2023

A Moment of Prose: Uncertainty

I wrote "Hold Both" and began to understand what I'd heard, what I'd read. No one can tell you what being a parent is like, how it feels to have a child inside you. regardless of the amount of love, with a parent in your home, outside the home, or you in theirs, no one can anyone describe, fully, this gestating grief and overwhelming stress of caregiving.

This is not normal stress. It's ongoing. It is *relentless.*

All the tools in the toolbox was never going to erase the stress. There would be no release from pain. There's no fixing the loved one you care for.

My mother's breast cancer is being starved, and disappearing. It does not change the trajectory her mind is taking, or her knees—and still, she's, relatively, physically healthy.

I cannot fix this capricious aging. Grief grows.

On a shopping trip, I put two jars of cherry jam into the cart for Mom's breakfast. Then a third. Mom's favorite Brown Cow Cherry Vanilla yogurt was getting hard to find, so I started getting jam to recreate it. She liked the yogurt on her morning granola, every other day. A spoon of jam. A spoon of vanilla yogurt. This worked fine.

I reached for a third, because, Why Not? And something in my mind said, "I won't need to buy more."

Yesterday I spooned jam from a fourth jar.

In the intervening weeks, I'd made mother start wearing compression socks—her feet and ankles swollen constantly. Her knees too painful to raise her feet to prevent this. I eased her fears of the future.

There is dread in demented confusion of her stories, in witnessing her pain, that she will be red in the face walking ten feet, and out of breath putting on her day gown.

But the jam prediction was foolish, born of a mind that needs certainty. All the events of gatherings, of family birthdays, and holidays—there is no predicting one event looming at an unknown remove. And yet...

I'm left with a calm, somehow.

I'm able to live just day by day. Each one a gift.

I don't need to know *some* date.

All I know is that I want her happy and safe. I want to do puzzles with her, even with the strange sing-songs.

I want to watch the Great British Baking Show, even if we repeat episodes—she can never remember there are three challenges each episode anyway, and she always finds each star baker as a win. I can be her companion, and help her be happy as much as her knees and arthritis can let her.

I cannot make her mind less unruly.

I cannot spare her pain.

I can change nothing... except continue to bring her joy.

Stress and Gestating Grief

I had assumed
That if I
Combatted
Controlled
Coped
With stress
It would evaporate.
There'd be peace.
I'd be an example
Of a good human—
Superhuman caregiver—
But this is chronic stress,
Something that doesn't
Fade into peace
With good coping skills.
It's not a one time thing
A flat tire on a lonely street,
But relentless days
Of stress growing
With each small sign,
Like a grief baby kicking
Or turning inside these walls.

I must make room
For this terrible stress
Let my body grow and cope
With the gestating grief
That comes
With the sounds of her aching bones
As she moves from bed to breakfast.

—Tuesday 25 July 2023

He Sang the Kol Nidre*

I kept the slippers
To contemplate
Her hoarding mind.
Grey velvet flats,
A line of fake diamonds
Along the heel.
A poof of marabou feathers
Upon the toe.
I helped her son bag
Unusual trash, rescue her clothes
Amid weird slippers
And size one negligees—
She at least a size sixteen.
He swore his elderly mother
Would never return to this
Hoarding house,
That she refused to let him see
Till broken bones in a car wreck
Forced the choice
On both of them.
Knee deep in the hoard,
He sang the *Kol Nidre*
For me with memories
Of him being a cantor.

The prayer sung upon the eve
Of the Day of Atonement
Filled the home
With peace and grace,
Blessing everything.

—Saturday 29 July 2023

* This happened at least a year before I moved into my mother's house.

We Grew Up Together

He's exhausted
With a full time job
And caregiving added on–
Even with his mother
Safe in a home,
There is no relief
With a mother at a remove.

She needed to be taken
From her home of hoarding
Where neglect let
Raccoons chew through ceilings
And steal food
From upper cabinets
And let the moonlight in.

There's an ache
At thinking
How our mothers–
A few houses apart–
Guarded their independence
Till either broken bones,
Or falls, like fate,
Stepped in.

His mother's only companions
To her self-enforced solitude
Were thieving raccoons
Who, of course
Could not help with the mess
No matter how often
They wash their hands.

—Saturday 29 July 2023

Her Best Friend

I sat with the woman
My mother calls her best friend,
But whom she never calls,
And never sees.

We spend another afternoon
Together, sharing poetry,
And then watch the memorial
Of her beloved niece,
Dead at seventy.

She lives with a canula
And a cord snaking through the house,
To help her breathe
And a more vibrant life
Than my mother who—
No doubt—is napping
In her chair, under the caring eyes
Of her hired caregiver.

—Saturday 29 July 2023

I Say It With Envy

Her son lives downstairs with his wife.
I've seen him once, and I know those eyes.
He worked harder than I do now,
For his father. The weight of worry remains
For his living mother—two years older than mine—
With half a lung, and other issues that brings
The weight of household care firmly
Into his hands.

She feels guilty in the night
That she took her son from all that he could be.
I know, he knew there was never
Any other choice but to come and care.
And we are twins in this.

I suggest, gently, that there's so much love,
Perhaps he and his wife can begin to emerge
From the sacred—and I know needed—
Privacy of their basement apartment and begin...
To live in the house that will one day
Be theirs—and help make changes to a house
Remarkably the same as when I visited as a child.
I know that she, and they, can grow as a family
Together, even now—altered, different, new.

And I say it with envy.

—Saturday 29 July 2023

Happy Images...Gone

She would sit
In her filth
Despite being in
A Nursing Home.
All those happy images
Of such places full of attention
And care... now rare.
Post COVID, the care
Is given by son and granddaughter,
Who use the Hoyer Lift,
The medical bed they bought,
And cannot bring her home
To too many stairs,
And not enough bedrooms.
The choices they make
Break the heart.

—Saturday 29 July 2023

Broken

Her wrist
Broken, pulled
All out of whack
Tangled and flung
By the Hoyer lift.

She wanted to change
Her beloved grandmother—
Give her a clean diaper—
Before she left for work,
The employee of the home
Who promised to help
Did not show,
So she tried it on her own.

She screams.
Her grandmother screams
And a resident
Came, finally, as fast
As his walker would allow,
And another mind, tangled
By dementia not far behind.

No nurses.
No attendants.
No employee of the facility
Presuming to give care.

A helpless old woman,
An old man shuffling
With a walker,
A kind soul with dementia
Helped the granddaughter
Who only wanted to make sure
Her loved one
Was clean—
Her wrist, now broken,
And her care now
At an end.

—Friday 4 August 2023

Bright, Bleak

The bright
Bleak
Tomb
Of my mother's home
Is where the dove
Comes to join
The brown finches
At the feeder
Is still
One of Waiting

—Tuesday 8 August 2023

Delay Grief

Delay your grief
And work on the puzzle.
Spend time with your mother—
For weeping won't solve
The lost pieces
Of her mind.
Yes, you just learned
There's one more duty
One more care:
You must manage even
The day and night pill box now.
She forgot when to take them.
So work on the puzzle
We lay upon the table
Between us.
Delay your grief,
And spend time with your mother.

—Friday 11 August 2023

Any Given Day

She tries to apologize
For being rude.
She doesn't like hurting
My feelings.
I try to tell her,
It's okay. There will be other...
Many other times and reasons
I will be upset.
I don't tell her I'm hurt
Almost every day.
I don't' tell her that
While, yes, anyone, anywhere
Can be rude, any given day.
I can no longer be angry
With Her.
I am enraged at her dementia.
For though she sees I'm hurt
She cannot tell why,
Nor can I tell her
That while I forgive,
She will, no doubt, forget.

—Friday 11 August 2023

Austenphile

I could tell you daily
The small things she forgets—
Small in some ways,
Like forgetting Darcy wrote Elizabeth,
Or the name of the woman
Emma 'adopted' as a friend.
It would not convey
Her Austenphilia. The antique copies
Three, four sets of series, old.
One new, and annotated,
The old copies from the 1900s
Worn down by her reading,
The spine taped up.
"Who is he writing?" she asks,
As we watch Ehle and Firth... again.
I explain, but later she adds,
"I've seen this so many times."
Which she has.
Such a small thing, this forgetting, till
Measured in the years of reading
Each book or enjoying their movies.
Books in her library fall,
One by one, upon me
With the weight of her forgetting.

—Friday 11 August 2023

Blessed Schedule

There's a strange
Almost autopilot
Where the schedule is the key—
But not the why.
That blessed schedule
Which calms aggravation
When the sun goes down.
A few times now it—
Not the event, or the joys
Of Nutella lunch,
Or the simple joys of a glass of wine—
Has left her face cheerfully blank.
She gets angry, almost,
That I'm not 'hopping to'
To respect the when.
She wheels her walker
With shuffled steps
Of a daily routine.

—Thursday 17 August 2023

Remains

I buy puppy and kitten stamps
For my mother: They will make her happy.
The supervisor of the post office
And I commiserate on aged parents—
Both his are gone. He tells me to treasure this time,
But breaks off suddenly, turning to another kiosk
"No, we can't!" he tells the woman with her package.
The woman protests; they're the only office
To deny her, when she tries to send mail.
Later I weep in my car for her.
The package the post office refused to send?
Cremated remains. I grieve, thinking it must be...
A loved one.

—Thursday 17 August 2023

Healthy?

There's no point
In being healthy
For this feels like forever.
I can't seem to gift my body
With once loved healthy foods.
Numbing seems the only option
Of any redeeming value.
For the drudgery of days and days and days
Of not going outside except
To mow her lawn, pull the weeds—
For it is inescapable: She needs...
More Care.
Just enough nutrition
To carry on, the forever of the day.

—Friday 25 August 2023

Fifteen

Perhaps I exaggerate
The fifteen minutes
It took for her to take
Fifteen steps—
Arms trembling on her walker
With effort to hold herself
Up. Knees bent as if to sit
Down. Ready to fall—
Refusing my help.
I'd have brought her wheel char
To her, but instead, finally
Unable to make her turn
At her favorite
Chair—I moved it
To her—Heavy swivel rocking
Easy chair
Where she could rest
After her excruciating
Journey

—Sunday 27 August 2023

Farragut

Meniscus, ACL, Nerves
Being ground down between femur and tibia
The patellas long migrated east and west.
Grinding, slowly losing the battle
To support her weight.
Still she struggled to walk, struggled to not fall...
Lifting one foot after the last
Finally unable to move her right foot
Under her, to turn to her favorite chair and relief.

A friend was there–
Our planned walk cancelled
As we helped support my mother at that last
Incomplete turn till
I moved her heavy chair
To meet her exhausted body–
She said: "This is not supportable."

Later, someone close,
Celebrating my mother's agency,
Quotes Farragut, "Dam the torpedoes, Full steam ahead.
He won the war."

I thought:
How could she say that?
Mom's boat has holes. It's already sinking.
And damn Farragut: There's no steam left anyway.

—Sunday 27 August 2023

Chronic Pain Dominates*

Even across the room,
Her grinding bones
Reverberates with me.
Mom stands, she gets to her walker,
She starts to move.
My twin, seeing my flinching face
Recommends: Distance, Reserve,
Claims that this is how nurses
Survive.
I flinch. Yes, this is my job
My role, my duty: to watch,
But I'm not a nurse,
Merely a daughter.
To listen, to care.
My twin smiles, claiming
She's tuned out the sound
Of our mother's tortured
Passing.

I cannot *but* feel alone
In all this unable to relate
To all my twin suggests,
To all that she must go through daily
When her own chronic pain dominates
Silently.

Compassion, resentment,
Sorrow, and loss thread
Passages through my heart.
I am no longer sure how
I might recover some
Connection
From the distance and reserve
How my twin recommends.

—Thursday 31 August 2023

* There ARE poems that challenge the suggested reserve, the concept of distance. It probably wasn't a bad one, but... hard to take when you're actually IN it.

Thank You, Lynda

"No,"
Was the reply
To my question.
No: I hadn't imagined it.
"By disagreeing with you
And maximizing
Your Mom's 'defiant spirit'
She minimizes her guilt
For doing shit to help."

When I speak of ordering
A medical bed sometime soon
She replies calmly,
"I assumed."

I recognize,
Suddenly,
Why this has always hurt
So much.
She is not sharing
In the daily grief and pain,
Tunes it out
To save herself,
With her own daily grinding life.

I think of the paid caregiver,
Seeing how Mom
Could no longer walk—
Holding me,
Silently weeping on my shoulder—
Her own fears, her own trials
Not preventing her
From sharing my grief
Sharing comfort and love.

—Thursday 31 August 2023.

My Sisters.

These are my feelings.
I do not know theirs—
Interpreting only what I
Am given between long moments
Alone,
With growing distance.
What do they think?
What do they feel?
My sisters.
I actually do not know.
In the solitary weeks,
Holding back sobs
When my fingers can feel
The vibrating of grinding bones
Beneath our mother's skin
As I help guide Mom's movements,
They change the tones
Of my interpreting ears,
Perhaps badly.

—Thursday 31 August 2023

Loving Kindness

I try to meditate
On Loving Kindness
But my grief is trebled.
My mother's increasing pain
Her diminish strength
Is braided with
The distance I feel
With my sisters—
The yawning gap
Where we misinterpret
Judge, misunderstand
Each other, and loving kindness
Is not found in the depths,
Except in a thread,
Like a lifeline, but...
So hard to find.

—Thursday 31 August 2023

Held Tight From the Past

I understand better now,
My sister's dreams held tight from the past...
Have no room in the reality here—
Mostly unseen, mostly un-experienced.
Those dreams, those hopes
Are running out of time to unfold
And are being outpaced by
Our mother's capricious aging.

—Thursday 31 August 2023

What is My Time

The clock doesn't tick
For constant care.
There's hours in that
Slow moving minute hand
That could be mine...

—Thursday 19 October 2023

What is Love?

Love, here...
Doesn't mean respect
Or 'I will protect
Your needs'...

Oh, wait, yes...
I do that.

She gives money instead.

—Thursday 19 October 2023

This is Normal

Her needs and fears
Take all her attention.
Of course. This is normal.
She is near helpless on her own.
And I am helpful...

Isn't it normal
To want things?
And then push them aside?
I must not lose myself
In the vortex
Of her very real needs,
The way I lost myself
Fawning from her feelings...

—Thursday 19 October 2023

Blue is for Boundaries

I put on the blue gloves
To wash my mother.
I had wanted to give her
The truth of human touch...
But beyond the need for intimacy
I need—more and more—
Some distance from this care.

—Thursday 21 February 2024

Part Five

Gravity

She never spins around
In her swiveling rocking chair
And yet I have returned to orbit
Around the weight of her needs
Bending my space and time

Spinning past my needs
I have long yearned
For an escape velocity
Trapped in this gravity well
With her needs so grave.

Must we meet the grave
Before my revolution
Outside of this spin,
Or find my life while shen
Gently rocks in her chair?

I let this question revolve
In my thoughts, for why
I feel held back from being
Not an extra arm, or legs
But a daughter with a life?

As she rocks in her chair
I have my own life downstairs
Where gravity is a weak force
Despite the constant calls
To remain in her orbit.

There is a resolve
Where I think of a solar wind
With their charged particles
And the tumult of their freedom,
And my own spinning energy.

The gravity of my plight
May be in part my own doing:
Forgetting my own energy,
Or the constancy of my passions

No need for velocity to escape this well
I am not creating my own grave,
But helping her,
While I find the means to live
And she grows closer to dying.

—Thursday 24 October 2024

A Moment of Prose: The Coming of Grief

The poems in this section lead up to and follow what happened starting the 20th of January. On that day, I noticed my Mom was listing to the right in whatever chair she was sitting on. I thought it odd. That somehow she couldn't hold herself up, even while sitting.

On the 22nd of January, she had two more falls. She was weak again—or *still was*, having recovered from COVID—having spent this day in her favorite spot, no longer her dangerous rocking chair, but a stable easy chair. First day not spent in bed.

I'd had to do more assisted pivot transfers. The last one, she couldn't do her part, and I wasn't strong enough to guide her alone. I helped her gently to the ground as she slid down my legs between bed and potty. I had to call 911 for assist.

Two hours later, I had to do so again.

I noticed—but didn't think much about it—but she couldn't seem to get her right leg to function. It was like that day she stopped using a walker. This, it would turn out, would be much worse. She was in her bed to stay.

On the 29th of January, we were expecting hospice care to bring us a hospital bed. This would get her out of the back room, and back to her favorite spot to see the bird feeder, and the neighbors walking past.

After she ate her cereal, I noticed that she couldn't seem to use her right hand—she's left-handed—to take her pills like normal. It was like a claw.

Uh oh! Was she having a stroke? I wondered, afraid.

I made her smile—and her face, her expression was even on both sides.

Curious.

We talked some more, discussed the color of her sheets for the new bed. While she was drinking coffee, she had a seizure.

I never want to see one again.

It was violent, and she gurgled like she was choking on vomit, and then listing to the side. I had to catch her head as she sank towards the edge of the bed and the spare two feet to the wall.

I couldn't seem to use my phone.

I thought, *This is why they tell you to practice.*

I'd been typing 911 on the pin part of my phone's opener, which of course it rejected. Then I suddenly saw the tiny letters: emergency. I hit it and dialed 911.

Later, after the first CT, even before their CTA, before the MRI, they knew it wasn't a stroke. There was, however, some anomaly in her left frontal lobe.

The doctors didn't know what had caused the inflammation in Mom's brain. It wasn't a tumor, rising up from her completely under control completely hormonal breast cancer. After the lumbar punch's test of the spinal fluid, there were no answers on why the inflammation was there, because it wasn't a bacterial or viral infection. She was too old for a sudden onset of an autoimmune disease.

And her symptoms were odd. She suddenly had pain in her right arm's joints, and then pain to the touch on BOTH legs. Which was gone the next day.

Her cognition was full of aphasia that she was actually aware of, and could fear—unlike the dementia that seemed so entirely normal to her.

On the 25th of February we finally had an answer that made sense of all the symptoms. Her brilliant GP shared screenshots of all the evidence, *but without personal details,* to her neurologist husband. He diagnosed Cerebral Spinal Fluid Cancer.

Without treatment—her choice, vetted by her doctor who had been having end-of-life choice conversations with her over the years—she had weeks, maybe months. Possibly days.

I Bring in Azaleas

The rhythms of my home
Included cold fresh spring air
Carried by rising bird song
Calling for the sun,
And the dancing delight
Of tree tops waking to the day.

My mother's house and world
Within four walls, shut windows
As she settles in her favorite chair
She claims: There's no bird song.

I bring in azaleas, white bright, and purple
From her own garden.
She delights, and I tell her,
"I'm bringing the world to you."
She will not go outside,
To feel this for herself, the sun
And wind, and listen to the birdsong.

It's hard to breath in this living tomb.

—Sunday 7 April 2024

One Minute of Bird Song

I bring in the sound
Of morning bird song
To a place so damp
And neglected as a tomb.
I cannot hold back
The damage of mistakes
I never made
Like shower tile on drywall,
And uncaulked windows.
I am too small to stand against
All that, and the world
The spreads from her rocking chair
Her placid presence filling
Her house like a hoard
But she laughs with delight
And the minute recording
Of morning bird song
Recorded on a dawn walk.
It reminds me of my home
In the mountains,
But even this small sampling
Cannot fill Mom's room.

—Monday 8 April 2024

She Relents...*

I had given myself away
When I knew my things
Could not really enter
Her house,
Not in the parts she could see.
Yes, I could bring them–
But shoved in the basement
Stored till needed (like me)
For three years, and more.

But soon, I will have
A garden, where a cabinet
Used to be.
One in the entryway
One behind a closed door
She never wants to open.
Hydroponics, for lettuce.
Maybe more?

And some paintings
Will come and replace
Some of hers.
And I can live in this house
And the memories of me
Aren't forgotten.
I can be part of the world,
Even HER world.
Maybe I can thrive.

—Tuesday 23 April 2024

* This took a sobbing fit—mine, not Mom's—a near tantrum because this year I had little relief in caregiving except the 18 hrs. from Visiting Angels. My sister could not come and help.

I was very lonely.

Expectations

The expectation of death
Has left...
She's sleeping late, and...
There's no fear,
Except for: The Now
And: What chores will I do
Today.

It feels strange
Who am I without imposing
Some emotional ideal
To my day?
To my caregiving?
What remains is love,
The hope of joy.
When will we laugh together next.
The eagerness of sharing
Our first lettuce greens from
Our hydroponic garden?

Bring the world into
Her confined life,
My confined life,
And I am alive, and with her.

—Friday 24 May 2024

Compass

Narrow the Needle to North
Towards waiting on Mom
A calmness, now, with more...
Happiness.

But what of my North?

—Sunday 26 May 2024

Ask and Have in One Direction

There's a quiet now
That once I had to fill
With noise—TV or wine,
Old books to re-re-re-read.
The battle within to fight
Or not fight against
A resolution echoed in the phrase:
"You're threatening me with
Assisted Living."
Something, mind you,
She already gets.
I must calmy say:
"It's not me. It's your knees.
And one day I might not
Be able to care for you."
I'd stopped battling with this
And within the cage of her—
Now seen clearly—
Unreasonable demands.
"I need you to practice
Assisted transfers."
If I can't help her—who will?

"I need time off."

—Friday 19 July 2024

Paid Time Off*

Four days at home...
And I see it:
All these plans for the future dreaming
Are like a gag
And a strait jacket—
Not intended to be placed upon me
But an old woman's whims
And the unrelenting lack
Of a future here.

No wonder I yearn
For my home—for that lush
Green, artistic, creative landscape.
It doesn't fit in a house
That's trying to reimagine itself
As a nursing home, or a mortuary
A place where life slowly fades
And is gone...

—Friday 19 July 2024

* Note on title: After about a year and a half, I had to demand time off. I had to ask for Mom to pay for it. We hadn't seen my sister in over a year. I was... exhausted. So the caregiver came for four days in a row, with my twin spending the night—a rare gift of her aid.

When I got back, my sister finally called to offer a longer stay back home.

Guilt or Free*

I put my foot down
So HARD
Mom's house ought to be
A crater.
There has to be a ME here...
And I have to declare
My limits
My needs.
It took days for her to see...
It became a shared goal.

I could see the wall
Where I'd no longer
Be able to give care.

A friend advised:
Make the choices guilt free
For a Home, or home
As she had, when her mother was
Aged 102.

—Friday 19 July 2024

* "102 and Linen" was written for that same elderly woman.

Reflections On...
Wednesday 22 January 2025

In her chair, wheelchair
Why is she
Listing to the right
And then...
After assisted transfers to and from
Too weak to stand,
I try to guide her
To bed, to rest,
And she slowly slides from me

Burly paramedics come
Once, and then again
Lifting her to her bed,
Her right side, I realize later...
She is unable to move.
Now, she is bed bound.

—Sunday 2 February 2025

Reflections On… Wednesday 29 January 2025

In the hospital
I dread breakfast.
I dread her holding–
If she even can,
With her dominant left hand–
Her cup of coffee.
Will she seize again,
Like she did five days ago?

It's not a stroke
But now, what does it matter,
This 'joke' about
The San Fransico earthquake or fire
'Which is worse'
Her right-side weakness
Her smile lopsided
Is it an infection inflaming her brain?

MRI displays a troubling brightness
With one curl of winding brain
Squeezing towards the right,
And a sliver of glow there too…

—Sunday 2 February 2025

30 Minutes to Myself

Why is it so hard
To take 30 minutes or less
To do yoga?
A new practice,
A few months old,
True...
Necessary to stretch
My injured hip from
Mom engineered (and faulty)
Transfers from her
Swiveling rocking chair.
Wake it up
For the duties of the day.
Me time
Useful in caring
For my mother.
To pull her up
To turn her once, twice
(Sometimes more,
As this is a new hard learned skill)
To change her, clean her,
Turn sheets, leverage
My own body weight...

But it's not just my body
That needs this time,
This yoga
It is my mind.
Can I just...
Focus on one thing
That's mine...

No. Not right now...
But I'll try again tomorrow,
For worry has invaded my mind
As a cancer destroys hers.

—Monday 10 February 2024

The Attending

She dropped information
Like bombs...
All other doctors shared information
Easily, no matter the difficulty
Padding the wording in easy to take tones
As they all struggled to find the cause of inflammation
In my mother's brain.
"It's malignant brain cancer..."
She says. And I think the neurologists said differently
For there is no tumor.
I fight back, bewildered, and shocked with confusion.

The next day, with nurses hanging bags of powerful
Anti-viral, for this has not yet been discounted.
"She's being discharged."
What? And the social worker
On her phone comes in saying the bed is on its way.
"No one's home!" I say.
And what the absolute fuck!
I can't take care of someone on an IV drip,
And who will be there to 'catch' the bed?
Nothing had been explained.

She might have apologized
For the first snafu,
Misreading the paperwork about amyloids
(Though... yeah, later, she wasn't far off track)
And had to send the neurologist and his assistant
To talk with me—and he
Made things clear, and understandable
Without any problem. Made sense,
And thus we could plan
For my mother to return home
"To be comfortable."

—Monday 10 February 2024

Even While She's Dying

There's joy in the living.
My cat's closeness, his purrs
Against my heart,
The life of the plants nearby,
The fresh memory of a friend,
Closeness, laughter, joy,
The memory of happiness—
The first in many weeks!—
Spending time with my daughter.

How could I?
With scans illuminating
The bright tension
In my mother's brain
Squeezing out use
Of her right side—
Her arm weak, her hand
Like a claw, but no stroke...
Bringing more dementia,
A black gift of more
Than aphasia, within
The curls of her brain:
There's more than confusion.
Sometimes there's fear.

She was never just this.
She was never just cancer
Or doom. Her smile, her laugh
Is not gone.
Her life. Her life. Her life
Had joy, has joy, has love
Intertwined in all things
Including her worn body
And abused brain.
I too want to bring her love
And joy—and feel it too—
Feeling it fuels me,
Energizes me more than caffeine
For the work I do,
Tending a dying woman.

Her body will lose this battle
Going on in her brain—
But she will be tended there
With love, with joy, with laughter
And friendship.
She will be carried there
In peace, and comfort.
For life—and death—was never
Just one thing.
There's joy in living
And will be till the end.

—Wednesday 19 February 2025

The Bonds of Sisterhood

I can't promise her that
We'll always get along,
That her daughters will
Love each other, and never
Fight again. Miscommunication
Runs a strong warp through
Our lives, whatever the weft
Weaves us into ourselves.
A few days of peace...
And it all seems to unravel
Again, with threading snarls
And trip wires to tangle me
Back into unhappiness
And grief—for the living
As well as what might linger
Once our beloved mother...
Is dead.

—Sunday 23 February 2025

Tin Type Eyes

There are times the light
Hits my mother's hazel eyes And
They have the grey, glassy
Light struck eyes of
Old tin type photos of the dead.
She smiles, and I'm glad
Wishing the blue-green
Were stronger than those
That reflect old photos.

—Sunday 23 February 2025

Framework

Routine
Is a framework
For her care—
Calming the sundowners,
Safety for the dementia,
And…
When "days, weeks…"
Has been said,
A course to guide
The volatile self—
Emotions that speed
Like a rollercoaster
Rage, exhaustion, tears,
Love, laughter, tears again—
Along the path
Holding us,
As we face her end.
The routine
The habit of the days
And we can just be—
And do…
And let go.

—Wednesday 26 February 2025

B12

My sister got angry
That following guidance,
I took out the vitamins
Among all the rest, but those for comfort
From my mother's daily medical
Regimen. 'Giving up', she thought.

After my sister left for her home,
After I read the doctor's notes
I realized that it was more
Than B12 I could take away;
Mom's blood pressure meds
Which I had left in.
A sleepless night thinking on
"She has been very consistent
With end of life wishes."
Requests I wasn't respecting.

Many of the meds were long term,
Big picture, prevention goals—
To prevent a stroke, prevent a seizure.
Yet cancer is taking over.
All that remains are comfort measures,
And a bitter and big a pill to swallow
As all those I'd taken away.
But the anger about B12,

Wasn't about giving up,
But loss, and what my sister risked:
The more lucid mother
Who talked for more than five minutes
Who showed her the love she needed—
To her mind, because of those
Very medications I'm taking away.

And following Mom's wishes,
Listening to her doctor's guidance,
It was, to an extent, *my* hands
That are taking it away—Except it's not,
For cerebral spinal fluid cancer,
Decided everything for us, anyway.

—Thursday 27 February 2025

Cathedral Colors, Revisited

I have paint chips
In my hands,
Broken shards, flaked off
From various graffiti artists' work
Barely hidden in a far too early spring
With blazing colors
On ruins of old water works in the woods
Some silver, against layers of pink
Blues, a red like umber,
And a speckled lime green.

I'm showing my artist daughter
The paths along these exploded, neglected
Ruins in a parkland beside train tracks
And we walk to paths under a road
To the Lullwater Water Tower by the falls.
It is so cool inside, with the Cathedral Colors
In a hot February day.
Graffiti has become a joy of watching change
Past the sorrows of once 'pristine' ruins.
Vibrant colors are mingled,
Or layered with change
So thin, like shards of mica,
That fall from the walls
And the memories of art now
Long gone.

—Friday 28 February 2025

Caring for Others

I'm tangled up
In all the demands
Family, my mother's friends
To make them feel safe,
Included, or contributing...
Offers of help that fade
As quickly as they're given
What threads hold me up
Within this snarl
I have to breath,
Find peace,
To see those friends who truly
Give, without the burden
Of such extended care.

Aren't I doing enough?
Already?

—Friday 28 February 2025

Dementia is Good

Yes,
Do lie...
Let her walk in 'now'
And the past twining together
In her bedridden wandering.
Let her forget
She's dying.
Hide what will come,
Not just pain, but...
More confusion.
Some I've seen
In hospital, when lost words
Frightened her
Whatever language
She was trying to use:
Dutch, Afrikaans, English
(Thankfully not the ones
I don't know,
Or barely understand)–
That it's *missing*,
That there is something very
Very *wrong*.
With dementia–
Not the cancer inflaming

Her brain—
It's *not gone*,
And hope and joy
Rises from wherever
She wanders.

Bring light into the room
Like opening the blinds
At dawn, or after she's clean.
Yes do lie, now
Let her feel whatever joy
She is left with
Because, right now,
Dementia is good.

—Saturday 1 March 2025

Foresight

No one can tell you when
Like asking a pendulum
Yes or No swings...
A friend once said,
'They're notoriously bad
At telling time'.
Well, doctors can't either.
Yet I wish they could,
Or that I had some
Clear, psychic layout
Of the coming days
To prepare myself,
To prepare Mom, to plan
Her care, yet left with
The knowledge
It might just come
Like a sudden seizure
After laughter and breakfast.

Maybe this is a better gift
Than foresight feels:
It must make me aware
Of the present.

Yes. Let Hospice
Tend to the future
They know so well,
They've seen so many times before
Leave me to spend my time
Caring and loving
My mother... Now.

—Saturday 1 March 2025

Sleep

The nurse asks,
Are you getting enough sleep,
The way friends ask
About my self-care.
And I have begun to think—
Not about green lit goals, but—
I have weeks left,
But there's a new gift
Of letting go:
Trusting the caregiver
(Or my sister,
When she comes)
Like never before,
Finding joy within
What is so very bleak.
For now, this is enough,
And I can walk in the woods,
To breathe,
To be me,
To be still, with a peace
That matters,
For it never feels
As if I've had enough
Sleep.

—Saturday 1 March 2025

Woodland Zen

The trees look like
Twisted pagodas
Of some forgotten forest.
Peace lingers here
Amid tangled branches
And fallen, decaying trees.
It is new, this peace
Away from the dying
Between the rot fed moss
Of my seat, and the
Sparling light of the lake
Screened by budding
Overgrowth of unloved privet
But I can detach enough
To sit, be still, breathe
Along this woodland walk.

—Saturday 1 March 2025

Capricious Cancer

There seems to be
Some kind of grace
Since Mom's been home
From hospital.
Is the diagnosis right?
Is there really some kind of cancer
Inflaming her brain, her spine?
She seems so... lucid now.
But her right hand
Continues to say: Yes it is.
There's still little other pain.

Yet the fluid flows
Up and down her spine,
Into her brain,
With cancer flowing and growing along.
Sometimes it blocks nerve endings
Sometimes not.
Her right hand doesn't hurt
Unless she moves it.

Mostly her mind is lucid,
But she could not place
A beloved former caregiver
Who came to visit, who came to help.
Guided back to memory,
My mother's joy increased,
And the sly gentleness of this cancer
I'll admit, I'm grateful
For its grace.

—Sunday 2 March 2025

Cruel, Kind Cancer

Her right hand,
Trembling, a bit swollen,
A bit blue...
She thinks she must have
Broken it.
It is the cancer
Flowing up and down
Her spine, in her brain.
First and still her hand,
Suddenly now, always,
Once both legs,
Now her back as well,
With the tense wait for more.
The cancer, cruel as it is,
At least had the kindness
To warn us of what
Is to come
In its bleak, and painful path.

—Monday 3 March 2025

God Answered...

I had prayed
That she would die
Before the pain came.
God answered without words:
That's what the morphine
Is for:
Ease the pain,
Gentle the passage,
Let love have time...
Whatever it is the cancer
Clearly still wants to do.

—Monday 3 March 2025

Memory that Lasts

For weeks I rarely
Saw the blue
Of my mother's eyes—
I'd only see something grey
Like daguerreotypes of the dead.
A few times she'd wake,
And her eyes were
Blue, and clear...
Like the spring sky after a storm.
"I'm a friend!" she once declared
Three days before she died,
And I said, "Yes, you are."
And with her bright eyes
Came laughter—daunted
By a lack of air, yet...
It could not take away
The purified pleasure
Of her delight, and her love:
All things she trusted, were true
Without demonstration, and...
Without the destruction of dying.

I will remember her face
Lit up with happiness,
Eyes bright and joyous,
Happy to see me, her daughter,
Stating, as if to everyone:
"I'm a friend!"
And a memory of love
That will last.

—Tuesday 11 March 2025

New Rules

I don't know
At all
What today will bring.
Cruel cancer laughed at us,
The day before,
Morphine took her pain away.
Yesterday, I tried to protect
Her right arm—
Now the whole limb,
Without touching it, moving it
Hovers at an 8 on the pain scale
And Mom says, stoic as always,
"It's okay."
I tried to turn her,
To change her,
And then everything hurt too much.
I laid her back down,
Not knowing what to do.
Cancer had changed its mind,
Flowing up and down her spine,
And does not want to play fair.

—Tuesday 4 March 2025

Fear shares much

She can't tell us
With morphine taking
Too far into sleep,
But when Jovina,
Her other caregiver,
Sat on the bed
To feed her some soup,
Mom flinched, cried out.
"Did I hurt you?"
Jovina asked, worried.
"Almost hurt..." Mom says.
This stoic, carful woman
Cannot always tell us she's in pain,
But she is afraid of it,
And this tells us much.

—Tuesday 4 March 2025

Better Guidance

Jovina and I agreed
We did not like this nurse.
I remember Donna telling me
About the parade of hospice nurses
Giving contradictory information,
While her own father was slowly dying.

Here it came in one 20 minute visit,
A litany of confusing conflicting advice
On the timing and amount of morphine
And other painkillers.
"Will you take my advice," he asks.
I flat out—and repeat it, each time he asks—
"No. I will not. I'll follow the advice
Of her charge nurse and supervisor!"

I was cheered to see Jovina's grim face
While he spoke. Taking myself away,
Hoping her uniform would speak
Of her experience, and authority—
Instead, he had her read the manual
Left, kindly, by the social worker,
As if she had none.

When he left, we hugged
Knowing we could tackle it all
Together, and wait for daylight
And a different hospice nurse
To give better guidance.

—Tuesday 4 March 2025

'Love' is so Inadequate

She wanted wine early.
At first, I put it off,
Then thought:
Freaking brain cancer*
She can have anything
She wants that it hasn't stolen.
She had wine,
I had an indigo elderberry G&T,
And we watched Firth and Ehle.
She ate three spoonfulls of soup,
And only half her favorite tiramisu—
I settled back
To watch the show, my mother...

THIS was what four years, four months
Was for.
Something the word 'love'
Was suddenly so inadequate for—
Yet, it probably was merely that: Love
And so special,
The years together, tending her
To this place, to this time.

All the frustrations, the sorrows,
The sense of loss...
Erased in this one moment.
However much time she has left,
I will be here for her.

—Wednesday 5 March 2025

* Actually it was Cerebral Spinal Fluid Cancer. It was easier for Mom to understand when she asked.

Anger washed away...

Those who went
Through this before,
Kept saying:
"You'll be grateful
That you had this time."

I would get so angry
Feeling only the burden,
That I carried...
Such weight!

Now?
I believe them.
In one minute looking at my mother...
I do feel
Only Gratitude.

—Wednesday 5 March 2025

Her Breath

Watching her breath
Is more compelling
Than a book,
Or a brief attempt at TV
She's not eating
Even on morphine
Her bowels are loose.
She talked about going to school
Here, and not...
I just want to watch her breath.

—Wednesday 5 March 2025

Part Six

Thursday 6 March 2025

"Who is it I am seeing?"
She asks moments after morphine
"It's Maria," I tell her,
"Your daughter, who loves you."
Just being here, for you, I think.
I hold her hand, smiling at her.
She still has the words.
She's glad at my smile,
And she makes a sound
Between sobs and laughter,
And not really either,
Carried by her ragged breath,
Slowly softened by slumber.

—5.05am

A Moment of Prose: The Last Few Days

At some point during the few days that came before, or that followed, my mother, one night before bed, struggled to tell me what she was feeling.

It was interesting to notice the difference between her dementia—which usually meant that something was gone from her mind—and the cerebral spinal fluid cancer, causing inflammation in her brain: She knew that there were words she couldn't reach for, no matter the language of choice.

"I'm afraid," she said, and then denied it.

She wasn't afraid of death itself, and so it took time to have that word, or the word anxious be paired with that lack of fear to what she was afraid of. She was afraid of what would happen, how it would happen.

Long before this, I promised that I'd always be honest with her. Yes, there were lately times when hiding the truth was essential. Not just by her choice, if she didn't want to know, I'd not say anything. Now, it was to keep her at peace. That said, if she did have questions about her dementia, or anything, I'd be as clear and forthright as she would wish.

So, when I understood what she wanted, I told her what to expect, between what would happen because she'd chose to be off oxygen, as well as what the cancer would to her experience of pain, her confusion. I promised that she'd have as much morphine as recommended by her charge nurse.

It took her even longer to admit that she didn't want me to be downstairs, ready to hear the bell—I'm not sure she even knew how to or physically could press that button to call me at this point. She also didn't want me to just be upstairs, in her old room, or the caregiver room.

She wanted me nearby. In the same room.

For days, I'd either sit in a chair where she could see me, watching TV with headphones, or reading, writing, and napping. When Jovina would come, my rock and (a truly perfect term for the caregivers and company) my Visiting Angel, I'd listen to a Yoga Nidra meditation, and try to get some rest, either in Mom's old room, or the couch.

This section of the book will have the days as "title" of the poem, and note the timing.

As it is her last days... it might be difficult for some caregivers to read.

My emotions, also, were raw, and so some of my words and feelings about my natural sisters are tempered by exhaustion, frustration, and often feeling alone.

I will say again that I do love both my sisters, and my eldest sister and I had many frank and open discussions that renewed love and care in a way some of these poems do not reflect. I've left them in, not to hurt her or my twin, especially as hope and love was there too. Those feelings were what I felt are also, apparently, all too common for caregivers in general.

Thursday 6 March 2025

Yes, it is true,
I don't want anyone here
Whom I have to take care of
Besides my mother.
Those who give care, yes.

I've felt that sharing
With Lynda and Jovina
Paid Visiting Angels
Who call her 'Mom',
My sisters in caring.

I don't want to go back
To sisters, when I seem to...
Always have to be careful
Of their feelings (and not mine).
Too many rifts too fresh
In their healing, to feel
As natural, as calm...

Yet my heart beats as well
In this selfishness.
It is not keeping them
From their mother,
Never that, really, But...

I see now, protecting my own heart
As our mother's death
Comes Near.

I think of the week before
When a friend made
One request too far...
And I wanted to throw my phone
Into the churning creek
Where I was walked,
On a very necessary break.
To silence the needs
And disappear away from
All these requests
For me to take care of THEM.

—5.40am

I call into hospice,
It is early.
Surely there's a nurse.
HE, the worst nurse,
Picks up, and I sigh.
I explain the timing of her last meds
And "Mom has a headache."
He replies:
"Sometimes morphine can
Give headaches.

Try Tylenol."
She can't swallow,
And I dread the idea of suppositories.
My first thought is:
You think it's the morphine?
What about the f'n
Cerebral Spinal Fluid Cancer?
I decide to wait,
Till a more reliable nurse can come.
Next time he answers
I'll just hang up,
And text her nurse,
Or the nurse supervisor.

—Around 6am

She woke up
And saw me.
I bent down.
Her face was joyous.
She said:
"I'm a friend."
I said, "Yes you are!"
And despite it being
More ragged-like
Breathing,

She laughed
With joy.

—10:40am

She asked Jovian,
With the bay window
Of the living room—
Her new bedroom—
Blazing with light,
So clear, so crisp
After the storms
The night before—
"Is it midnight?"

—Noonish

She wakes. She asks us:
"Are there more men here?"
Jovina and I are surprised.
I pause, listing in my mind,
All the men friends
Who might come at a call.

"No," I say. "Why?
Do you want some?"
She laughs,
And then falls back asleep.

—3:00pm

Sometimes
She breathes
And it sounds
Like sobs
She's too tired
To express,
And there are no tears.

—8:00pm

(The nurse had come,
And told me her heart was racing
And it would not be long.)

I hold the hand
That lays upon her chest

Her heart
Is beating
So fast,
Working so hard
I don't need
A stethoscope...
I can feel it
In my fingertips.

—9:00pm

I'll no longer
Be afraid.
I will begin
To tell her:
Goodbye
Along with
I love you.

I list her
Daughters
Granddaughters
"We all love you."

—9:30pm

Friday 7 March 2025

Her breath
Used to sound
As if she
Were running
A marathon
Just to put on
Her socks.
Now her heart
Races with effort
Of dying.

Sometimes
She looks
So small
In this Hospice bed
Like a little girl
Curled up
Under the blanket
She's had
Since she was eight.

—12:30am

I feel so much more at peace,
Now that I've said goodbye.
Let the noise come.
People.
They cannot now
Destroy my peace.

—Around 2am

Jovina, the caregiver,
Thought she was dizzy,
Sitting in the chair,
Holding Mom's hand
While I rested on the couch.
Surely Mom wasn't shaking that much!
No need for a stethoscope,
No need for a gentle hand
Upon hers...
Her heart
Working so hard,
We now could see it
Shaking her body to the beat
Of her exhausted heart.

—4:00pm

Chronic Pain Addendum

Detatchment
Must be a virtue,
I think now.
Perhaps
I can see
My emotions were so...
Reactionary, so intense
My sister's advice
Was kindly given.

—Around 4:30 to 5

Saturday 8 March 2025*

I don't even know
What time it is:
I remember my elder sister
Sleeping on the couch
Of the living room
Where Mom's hospital bed
Had been...
Exhausted from the drive
Waiting as Mom's exhausted
Heart and lungs worked.

My sister...
We'd had such conflicts
These past few years
Accusations of abuse,
Feeling trapped, fighting out
As if from an impossible situation...

Yet there she sleeps.

I'd watched our mother's heart race
Shaking her whole body.

My sister napped till...
Her heart went quieter, and lungs
Took on that ragged marathon towards death.

Holding hands, holding hers,
Apnea giving several lies to "Now"
Till her beating heart and breath
Were done at 12:54am...
Which was not legal till the nurse
Could pronounce.

Our sick mother
Was no bond of healing
Honesty, months prior, and now this...
My sister, my friend, my refuge,
Companion to the dying woman
Whose hands we held between us
In those final moments.

* At this point, I didn't record the time I wrote the poem. The death certificate listed it when the nurse came to record it officially. I figured out what day it was, only be checking my phone. From 4pm till past her death, it was as if time was 'now' and forever.

Tuesday 11 March 2025

Three to four days
Later
It's still a blur,
From days of only naps...
And the minutia of planning
Post death began
To overwhelm.
Nearly broke me.
My sister took over,
But now,
She speaks of Thank You cards
And a sense of obligation...

Yes, it *is* just polite
But now we have to be careful
Of everyone *else's* feelings?
In case we miss
One donation, one visit
One bunch of flowers?

Oh God...
It's just so much *work!*
Haven't *I* done enough?

Haven't *we?*

The hospital bed is gone.
Mom's favorite chair removed
Long before. I sit here,
In a different chair now,
Where she used to be.
The house still somehow...
Familiar. The family home,
And I know no exile anymore
Because I get to *be* here,
In a way I was not
For more than four years before?
There's no loss—for she feels
Present in all that she made,
And I am here too
But daughter,
Not caregiver, an intrusion
Into the solitude she valued
As filling the space with memories
Of friendship, family, the past.

Maybe my eldest sister
Has made this all so
With writing the obituary,
Arranging the memorial,
While I catch up on sleep...
For it feels as if the rooms of this house
Are filled with the concept of family
Though, now, neither father nor mother
Will ever walk through this space again.

Wednesday 12 March 2025

Maybe my body
Does know, and my mind
Has yet to catch up.
It feels alert to go,
At the sound of a bell,
Like a runner to a shot.
My dreams are of violence
Like terrorism and breaking glass
Not this thing...
That happened to me,
Watching death rattles and
And erratic breathing,
Or apnea teasing towards the last.

Her only communications
At the end, were of love,
Of joy, of expectation...
Not the terrible pain that was due

I doubt this gratitude
Will fade, replaced by some evil.

Grief will come and dance
With this unexpected partner.

I don't have to be
In the basement
Anymore—I can live
In the whole house
My sister being here
Has helped make this
Happen, Yet I can tell...
I crave the day I can
Be here alone. Maybe then...
I can weep for what
I lost.

Grief
Must step back
From all
The minutia
Of paperwork
Signed not once,
Not twice, now three times

Delays for the
Death certificates
And all the planning
And all the friends
WE must comfort, protect feelings for.
Grief will come—
Yes.
Of course—
But not till we
Are done with the paperwork.

Thursday 13 March 2025

She paid for cremation...
But apparently even so,
It's unfinished by dying.
We have to sign. All of us
Mentioned in her health
Directive, giving no direction
For this at all... Signed once
At the funeral home, then
Twice, then thrice... For
The agent had us all sign
In all the wrong lines.

Wednesday 19 March 2025

So many empty hours
With a different weight
Than waiting upon her.
My twin coming for dinner,
Said *It feels like*
A family home again.
Mom had filled her space
With her own energy, needs...
Even those rooms given
Over to me, my use,
An exile no longer exile:
Familiar again

Is this some kind of grace?
A reprieve from grief?
Or will those empty hours
Crash upon me at some later date?

Why am I surprised
That writing
And editing

Help me feel
Like myself?
That I needed this
More than trees
Walks in the woods
Or yoga.
If I return to myself...
Maybe I will grieve.

A neighbor thought
I was a nurse,
Because... merely because
I was a caregiver.
"How do you do that?"
She asked, amazed.
Like any daughter or son
Called upon to do the work,
You learn, the hard way,
And hope that the fears,
Exhaustion, the sorrow
And grief don't line your face
Weigh down your shoulders
For everyone to see...
Because there's no training
Except by doing.

Friday 21 March 2025

I think I had believed
That grief would be
Some outside thing
Like a lost hug, or smile
Seeing my mother's empty chair
Not some inside thing
Like a fountain
Of clear water rising up
To drown me
In a flood of tears.

Wordless, definitionless flood
Poured me onto the floor
Carried me through
The rocky streams of my sorrow.
Grief is an inside thing.

I had thought
It would look different,
Feel different,
Recognizable by something I'd read
Or seen in some movie.

Where were the words
To describe these feelings?

A dictionary of grief
Should help me process
My mother's passing...
Right?

All the books in my library, or hers
Cannot tell me, show me
This thing called grief.

All I can do is shut those books,
Turn off the TV
Let go all the false bravery
Of any dictionary terms,
And let myself just FEEL it,
Without definition,
Without lines, or boundaries
Knowing that even
These words I write,
Won't display it.

Saturday 29 March 2025*

I was so much
Alone
With my mother
For so long.
Who are these people
To take such a full share
Of grief for her passing?
She was a friend
To all of them,
Once,
A surrogate mother
A kind wife
Of her professorial husband.
88 and a few months
She filled parts of their lives
Like she filled this house
From her favorite rocking chair.

I'm resentful.
I want them gone.
Away.
Forever.

But they loved her too.

* This day would have been my mother's 89th birthday. It was the day of her memorial.

The End

Home now,
I recover my neglected home,
Return to the lost parts of myself,
Discover a *new* self,
Like a last gift
From my beloved mother.

—Thursday 5 June 2025

About the Author

Mab Morris lives in Dahlonega, Georgia, with a number of cats and a Celtic labyrinth of her own design. Her storytelling and her love of fantasy began at a very young age, where she was drawn to Ursula K. Le Guin and J.R.R. Tolkien. Mythology, history, and folklore are her passion.

She writes mystical fantasy books set in the past, present and future of the world of Ihyel, where demi-gods and mortals alike struggle with their fate. She also writes the murder-mysteries of The Bone Reader, about Cemirowl who speaks with the dead, and the Regency adventures of gender-fluid spy Alex Goodward.

Check out www.mabmorris.com for more info.

Other Books by Mab Morris

Cemirowl is gifted, and cursed. She sees the spirits of the dead, and sees the future in her basket of bones; her sight is cryptic, lacking, and mostly useless. In her tiny village, she is a priestess, but still an object of curiosity and an outcast.

A chance meeting brings one of the king's caballiers to her door for a reading, for nothing more than some entertainment. He is well-entertained indeed by her predictions of his lady loves… and far less so when she foretells a coming death. He leaves, dismissing her. But for all that her power is mysterious and often confusing, it is never, ever wrong.

When Queen Tidyri is murdered, the caballiers return for Cemirowl. She is brought unwillingly into the palace and into a web of intrigue and lies, where King Larthor rages in his grief. He demands that Cemirowl now use her gifts to find the one who killed his beloved wife.

Cemirowl must draw on all her abilities – her powers, no matter how unreliable; her intuition for reading people; her knowledge; and her wits – to discover the murderer, lay the spirits of the dead to rest, and help the living to grieve and find peace. And, perhaps, she will finally find a place where she belongs.

LOST BONES is a fantastical murder mystery set in the rich world of Ihyel, where the hard-won peace between two kingdoms rests on the shoulders of one determined, compassionate priestess.

The world is changing, perhaps not for the better.

The Doctor-Diviners, keepers of old lore and healing, are fading away as their craft is usurped by Science. Soon the workings of Medicine will be guided only by rationality, and the mystic arts of divination and calling out to the ancestors will be lost. The lowly apprentice and foundling Sen is one of the few who sees the value of the old ways, and seeks to preserve them. Raised by Grandmother Turani in the woods and speaking the old Ndeb tongue, she is skilled in her craft and diligent in her study.

But her path to becoming a Master Doctor-Diviner is interrupted when a chance meeting reveals her parents may not be unknown. The Lady Ravantha - brooding, damaged, and dangerous - believes Sen is her lost daughter. Sen believes otherwise, but visions of the past torment her dreams and unsettle her waking. And always, always, Jackal and Crow mock her with their laughter at how much she does not yet know.

Sen of the Woods wants nothing of the life being chosen for her, but she will have to step carefully around Ravantha. For she is a healer above all, and she will not ignore someone in pain.

APPRENTICE is the first in the trilogy of Sen of the Woods, about one life's fight with fate and destiny.

The year is 1800, and England is not a kind place for a woman on the brink of ruin. For Alexandrina Goodward, escape can only mean subterfuge. She takes the persona of Lilly Green and vanishes into the countryside, with the help of her supposed aunt, Mrs. Green, and her occasionally ditzy brother.

But the deception, and the risk, rises to another level when Alex is forced to take on a new persona in order to keep her new household running. She becomes Alex Goodward, a well-read and scholarly man, with the help of

Mrs. Green, a new set of clothes, and an old wig. It's more than a disguise; HE is Alex, as much as SHE is Lilly.

Alex keeps up the ruse out of necessity, knowing that the past still looms over them all. Her name has been written into a ledger of secrets, one that could end her life and ruin all of England. As Lilly Green, she is defenseless. As Alex Goodward, he can join a magical coterie of men dedicated to finding the ledger and keeping its secrets out of the wrong hands.

Chasing the ledger will lead her into the halls of Cambridge, into the underbelly of London, and into the arms of a Russian prince. But Alex Goodward, whether a man or a woman, is a rare breed, and he's more than ready for the task of defending the Crown.

ALEX GOODWARD AND THE SECRET LEDGER is the first adventure of a gender-fluid spy in Regency England, where the bounds of male and female are blurred in order to protect the innocent.

www.ingramcontent.com/pod-product-compliance
Lightning Source LLC
LaVergne TN
LVHW100256210926
848480LV00003B/939
9798995192640